The First Eighty Years Are the Hardest

Feeling, Dealing, Healing

Mary Roush

Special Note:

My mother, Mary Roush, completed the manuscript for this book just a few weeks before her sudden death in 2012. On August 25, she experienced sudden extreme abdominal pain and fainted at the table just before her Saturday morning AA meeting was to begin. One of her many beloved AA sponsees followed the ambulance to the hospital and stayed with her in the Emergency Room for the next several hours as family members were notified. Mary barely survived emergency surgery later that afternoon to repair a perforated bowel. She never regained consciousness, though, and she passed away peacefully on the evening of August 27, 2012.

I have taken Mary's manuscript and a few of her many selected photos through to the printing and publication stages as I believe was her final wish.

Please feel free to contact me with any questions through my self-development blog, www.MovedandShaken.com.

Copies of this book can be purchased from Amazon, CreateSpace, and through the blog/website designed to celebrate the life and work of Mary Roush, www.Feel-Deal-Heal.com.

This site includes a Photo Gallery, more background information, and several of Mary's academic reflection papers about women and alcoholism, addiction and family treatment, and codependency. We welcome your comments and questions.

Kris Roush

DEDICATED TO SKIP

*Your loving support the last 60-plus years has
been "the wind beneath my wings."*

I love you now and for always,

Mary

Praise for *The First Eighty Years Are the Hardest: Feeling, Dealing, Healing*

"Mary Roush is someone you should know, and if you did not have the opportunity to do so while she was alive, it's not too late. Her spirit lives on through her family, friends, the myriad of people she touched throughout her life, and her own words in her forthright, inspiring memoir, The First Eighty Years Are the Hardest. Mary tells her life story of childhood challenges, health problems, and near death experiences that ultimately dropped her off into the abyss of alcoholism. Her book is truly about learning how to feel, deal, and heal. Without anger, bitterness, or victimization she guides us through her life of recovery, forgiveness, and unfolding wisdom. Her story offers an opportunity for all of us to rediscover the healing grace within our own being. Mary will always be treasured for her passion and compassion, kindness, generosity, and courage to keep trying until she got where she wanted to go. And arrive, she did! No wonder so many of us love and appreciate her. Godspeed, Mary."

—Sandy Brewer, Ph.D.
Author, *Pursuit of Light: An Extraordinary Journey*

"Mary magically takes us through her eighty years of ups, downs, joys, pains and life. From her vantage point of age eighty, she identifies her feelings at each stage of life and each event so we can know her better than she knew herself at the time. Bits of important information from early years foreshadow events to come. More than a narrative, "The First Eighty Years Are the Hardest" is a journey any of us can relate to and learn from. Mary, you were the best!"

The following excerpt is one of many profound pieces in her story:

> *"I feel a heartbeat!" The baby had survived. Having been schooled in Catholic principles and church laws, I remembered that in such a case as this, if it's a question to save the child or the mother, the child is the priority. And I was in a Catholic hospital. I believe that God directed me to come back from that near-death experience in order to resume my maternal duties and ultimately work to complete the task of finding my own life's purpose. It was also, eventually, one of the factors that influenced my later distancing of myself from the Church.*

—Dawn V. Obrecht, M.D.
Author, *From the Edge of the Cliff: Understanding the Two Phases of Recovery and Becoming the Person You're Meant to Be*

"The more I read, the deeper my trust evolved, allowing me to take an honest look at my own feelings. I could sense Mary's vulnerability and courage as she took on her life events and then deeply understood that giving back was so much a part of her healing. This book is now a valuable addition to my life in recovery. Thank you, Mary Roush, for sharing so honestly."

—Mary Wakefield

"Mary is a born story teller. Her warmth and openness gives others permission to begin healing their own lives. Her story is to be treasured. Important words at an important time on the earth."

—Tina Powers,
Intuitive, Author, *Reporting for the Other Side*

∽

"I have had the extraordinary gift of Mary Roush as my friend and guide in my day-to-day life. Her voice in this writing is so strong and true that it feels like one of our many conversations. What a courageous gift of honesty it was to write it all down! Because she made the effort to know herself and share that knowledge, she is still here and continuing her work of helping others on our own journeys. Mary is an example of how a courageous person can turn adversities into assets. She used her pain to open herself to love. And further, she has shared that love she received and gave it generously to all the people in her life. For everyone who reads this book, you will receive a great gift – the honor of knowing Mary. I know she will touch your life."

—Susanne

∽

"What a legacy Mary Roush leaves us with in the writing of her beautiful book! Her courage is remarkable and inspiring. As a woman and as a "friend of Bill W.," I found great comfort in Mary's spiritual journey of awakening. Her talents as a counselor, teacher, and visionary are a healing force for others seeking recovery. Through her commitment to her own wellness, she has served like a pebble tossed in still waters, rippling out and touching the lives of many people who continue to touch more lives in an engaging dance of "feeling, dealing, and healing!" Thank you, Mary"

—Carmel Merryman
Life Coach, Live Your Life Now Coaching

∾

"Here is the remarkable journey of a daughter, sister, wife, mother, grandmother, and a recovering woman. Learn from Mary's struggles, overcoming adversity and thriving as a gifted therapist who clearly saw, early on, the need to focus on families and children. I have been so blessed to call Mary my friend."

—Jerry Moe, MA
Children's Counselor

TABLE OF
CONTENTS

Acknowledgements

For many years, many friends and family members have urged me to write "my story."

With the calendar reminding me of my oncoming birthday with an eight-zero attached to it, the thought to actually put it all down on paper came from an increasingly louder voice within me...so I am just following directions.

Reflecting back, I know how deeply I treasure and love my dear, Skip and our over 60 years of growing up in life together.

The ultimate joy has been the honor of being allowed to be the mother of Karen, Kathy, Kris, Kimberly, Mike, and Kay! They all had to endure many years of Skip's and my "growing pains." We have all celebrated, cried, laughed, and loved, despite those dark years, but today we are all survivors...victors! And, we are family.

So today, I dedicate this book of memories to them all, as we each experience the results of each of our transformations, struggles, and successes.

I love you all!

Mary/Mom, August, 2011

PROLOGUE

"Think...Think...Think" That was a sign on the wall across the table from where I sat at an Alcoholics Anonymous clubhouse in suburban Philadelphia. "What does that mean?" I wondered. What was a "lady" like me doing in this shabby room above a bar, accessed by the fire escape steps outside the back door? The smell of coffee and cigarette smoke permeated the room. I noticed other worn-looking signs spaced across the wall: "Easy Does It," "Keep it Simple," "First Things First," "Let Go, Let God." My heart sank when I heard the word, "God," as I knew I was so bad that God had given up on me long ago. And then I thought, "I don't even belong here." As I started to leave, a man named Sam (later I learned he drove a Yellow Cab in City Center) must have sensed my discomfort and gently reassured me that I needn't be concerned about the sayings or their meanings, promising that if I would stay and listen to others ahead of me on their own road of addiction recovery, that someday I, too, could look happy and actually laugh again. "Impossible," I thought as I had been put off by the sounds of joking and laughter by some men convening around the coffee maker. I agreed to spend another two hours before driving back home before my six children returned from school. More people, mostly men, joined the rest of us at the ash-tray filled table. Others took chairs, theater-style, that reached to that magic coffee elixir inside the back door. Soon, a well-dressed, nice looking man took his place at the head of the table and I was present for the first meeting of Alcoholics Anonymous of my life. He read something from a "Big Book" and then started the discussion of a topic which was then open for other members to share their opinions on how that topic related to their own lives. Ninety minutes later, my head was full of voices, experiences, and stories of encouragement, and I noticed people seldom talked about wanting to drink. They were talking about living a life free of the alcohol and pills that had driven me to the depths of my own hell. My outward appearance as "The Executive's Wife" and suburban homemaker belied the shame, guilt, and hopelessness raging inside, subdued only by more of the substances that had brought me here in the first place. Certainly, *someone* might be able to help me stop this craving and daily struggling, to no avail, to not pick up that first drink, even a little sip that ultimately led to the bottomless glass. That liquid ice would calm the heat that made those twisted knots in my stomach untie.

> "Beginnings are apt to be shabby"
> –Rachel Carson

As I rose to leave, several people, even the few women there, smiled and encouraged me to come back the next day and just not pick up the first drink in between. They even gave me their phone numbers I could call if things got too tough. But the thing I remember most as I headed down those fire escape stairs to my car, was the echo of voices, "See you tomorrow, Mary." I heard my own name in a loving tone by people who seemingly wanted to help me! I had become so busy becoming someone else's "something" role, I had lost <u>me</u> many years before. *Me...Mary.*

Over 40 years later, I look back and can picture and feel myself in that room again, "Sick and tired of being sick and tired," as they say. I was finally at my "bottom," willing to listen and follow directions. In the ensuing years of growth in sobriety, both personally and professionally, I have come to much better elaborate on the "Think" caution and have added my own hard-won slogan: "Feel, Deal, Heal." My best thinking had kept me locked in my head, intellectualizing, rationalizing, and blaming. I had ignored the other two thirds of my body from the neck down, with a heart full of pain, loss, fear, anger, shame, inadequacy, guilt, low self-worth, etc... Feelings! Since I had never learned a vocabulary for them (no-one talked about anything inside them; it was always about "doing" rather than "being"). And ladies were certainly never angry, but always presented a smiling face to the world. I wore a competent, responsible super-woman mask as I mothered my six children (five of them girls), making sure that they too, always looked their best, and knowing I was to teach them to be "ladies" and my son, Mike, a "gentleman."

> "A baby learning to walk falls a lot"
>
> –Kathleen Rowe

But, behind the mask, there was hidden the shame that I was not really the model "lady" they should emulate. I was a sinner and doomed to hell as the nuns had so faithfully taught me. So there was really no God to turn to. I was not good enough. Even in the early days of my AA experience, when, alcohol and pill-free,

Feelings of sadness would come up in tears (Feelings), the men (the "keepers" of the Program - not many women then) would tell me I was allowed only two minutes of self-pity a day, and I had just had them! Little did anyone know my tears were a healthy, necessary response to all the losses I had incurred (besides my drug "fixes"), and I was grieving. I was <u>Dealing</u> with my Feelings even though I didn't understand all of this at the time.

> "Edge up to your pain and give it a name"
> –Patricia Benson

Today, I know I have been Healing from all that painful abuse: mental, physical, emotional, spiritual, and social. This is my story.

CHAPTER 1
1931-1951

FEELING

"Your Daddy's dead." These were Aunt Carmen's words as I sat on her lap in the sunroom of our home in Duluth, Minnesota. My little brother and I had just returned to our house after suddenly being taken away by good friends of my parents a few days earlier. I hurried to see mommy, but she was lying on the couch crying and all my aunts and uncles were sitting around quietly, many of them in tears. When I heard those words, I thought I had better cry too, because something sad had happened but I didn't know what "dead" meant. Daddy had gone on a camping and fishing trip to the Lake of the Woods in Canada with some of his brothers a few days ago and I remembered walking with him and mommy to the street car, and he waved good-bye to mommy, Bobbie, and me. The other thing I remembered was waking up one night, hearing my mommy talking on the telephone, and she was twisting a dish towel nervously around her hands. The word "missing" was about my daddy. But until that day in our sunroom, I had only one vague memory of being in a strange house, looking up at a pretty lamp on a table as high as I was. It was July and I was going to start 1ˢᵗ grade in the fall. I had loved Kindergarten, and had such happy memories of taking walks with my daddy after dinner in the evenings, telling him about my school day, looking up at his twinkling eyes as I grasped his hand. And of course, we had such fun sliding down Duluth's hills on our toboggans the past winter.

(My daddy, Adolf Leslie Shay (Skjeie) married my mother in 1929. They named each other "doorknob" and "hinges," as he wrote: "Then, together we can open the door to true happiness." I was born in 1931 and my brother, Bobbie, in 1935).

Even more recently, daddy and I had gone down to the Lake Superior shore and I watched him as he swam out into the cold water. I was so proud of him and the trophies he won in swimming meets. One of our favorite games was when he would dive underwater out of sight, and as I anxiously watched for him to return, I would hear his voice calling, "Here, Mary Helen!" way over to my side where he had swum underwater. "Oh daddy," I would laugh, "you surprised me!" We were pals and I felt so secure with him.

My next memories were of being on a train with mommy and Bobbie, on our way to Columbus, Ohio where my grandma and grandpa Nilssen and their son, John (then in high school) had moved. Grandpa's harness, leathers, and saddle manufacturing company in Duluth had had to close because of the Depression and he had to leave his Norwegian immigrant families in Minnesota and Clear Lake, Wisconsin and take a job far away and start a new life in Columbus. Somehow, in all of this confusion, I heard snatches of conversations about drowning in that lake in Canada. The body finally washed ashore four days later, nothing I could really understand. I just knew my daddy was gone and every familiar part of my life disappeared. I have no memory of anyone ever talking about my father or what had happened.

In September, I started 1ˢᵗ grade in a Catholic school and began what was to be a lifetime friendship with Peggy, whose family lived near my grandparents' home. I felt different though. Everyone else had daddies but me. But I knew, deep inside, that daddy was just hiding underwater and that he would come back and surprise me like he used to. I would lie on the grass and watch the clouds or the stars for which one kept my daddy hidden from me. And that is when my life's recurring dreams began as I searched everywhere I learned about in Geography class, looking for my daddy.

> FEELINGS: (buried) I had not been at the funeral and burial which had taken place before I returned home to my Aunt Carmen's lap. I had been "sent away." I surmised, what did I do wrong that I needed to leave? My daddy always came back from the water. Why not this time? What did I do wrong? Guilt, grief, loss, abandonment, simmering anger, - and, internalized deep in my soul, - unconscious shame and guilt.

The playground across the street became my home away from the new house grandpa and my mother bought soon after our move to Columbus. From here, I could walk the eight blocks back and forth to school where I learned to fear and respect those women in the cumbersome habits of the Franciscan nuns. The Catechism talked about "God," something I knew nothing about, but the first question said, "God is Love" and He made me to be a good person in this life, "and be forever happy with

Him in the next." But my daddy couldn't be there because he was going to come back like my friends' daddies and we would take walks and laugh at the cartoons he used to draw. Uncle John had gone into the Army after the Pearl Harbor tragedy. He spent four years in the New Guinea jungles. The war was what everyone talked about, and pictures in the newsreels at every Saturday matinee at the Indianola Theater talked about men being killed and bombs destroying peoples' homes in some city called London. "The War Effort" made everyone feel needed and important and my Campfire Girl troop helped assemble those ever-present "ration books." Then, in 7th grade I joined the Navy League Volunteers with other young girls to train to be nurse's aides in local hospitals because so many nurses had "gone to war." And because so many high school boys had gone away to fight, I was one of the girls to take a paper route and pull my wagon of papers to house after house, and I had to learn to collect and make change. It was a confusing time for children, especially living in a house where mommy didn't get home from work until after Bobbie's and my bedtimes. We three lived in the master bedroom on the 2nd floor of that house with a double bed and big chair that unfolded to make a bed. Grandpa had his own bedroom and grandma moved into the room John had left. Later, when I was in 8th grade and my hero uncle returned home, he took back his former room so grandma chose to sleep on the living room couch. When I practiced my piano lessons, she demanded perfection, just as when I vacuumed the rug and dared to miss one little thread!

During those years my mother began a career in Civil Service and worked at a local Army Base where one of her duties was to send letters to parents of sons who had been "killed in action." Then those blue-starred window hangings they displayed in their windows were replaced by a gold star, the ultimate sacrifice. Some daddies of my friends also went to war, so sometimes

I didn't feel so alone in my strange combination family. Grandpa was a quiet hard-working Norwegian who made his special buttermilk pancakes every Sunday morning. Once in a while, he would let me go to his work where he had a whole floor full of leathers for horses, saddles, and harnesses. And I can still remember those distant leather smells as I watched him at his enormous roll-top desk. Because of his connection with "horse people," he was able to arrange frequent opportunities for me and my friend, Lorna Lucas, to do a great deal of riding. I even got jodhpurs and a crop!

Although I didn't know about such things at the time, grandma had sunk into a deep depression after all the losses of their former affluent and social lifestyle in Duluth. Now I can better accept and understand why she was so difficult to live with. Most of the time she spent sitting at the corner of the davenport, grieving for her son, fretting, worrying, waiting for any mail, letters with so many holes in the paper where censors had reviewed and determined the safety of any soldier's personal information.

Later in my life, I learned that to the degree a person feels inadequate inside, the more they become the ultimate perfectionist to the outside world. As a child, growing up with grandma as the only adult presence in the house five days a week, there was a tight rein on Bobbie's and my natural child's curiosities and temperaments. There could never be a glass of water enjoyed in the kitchen without immediately washing, drying, and returning the glass to the cupboard. Grandpa had fixed up a playroom for us in the basement with a porch swing and a big table where we could spend hours working on jig-saw puzzles. Then grandpa would frequently glue the pieces together to hang the pictures on the concrete block walls. Grandma would often lock us down there. I remember hours and hours spent listening to records on the old Victrola under the basement steps. *"March of the Toys," "Babes in Toyland,"* and all those records of Enrique Caruso (a favorite of my grandma's), and my imagination would soar with that music! A set of picture encyclopedias exposed me to a world of different cultures, and unique, far away countries' custom clothing. Oh, and I remember learning more about places outside Ohio! Grandpa would often travel, selling harnesses and saddles and he would bring back stacks of picture post cards of glamorous, exciting places from all over the United States. I would sit on the floor and stand them all up to make rooms and passageways. I especially remember pictures of the Wrigley Mansion on Catalina Island, and of course, related it all to my favorite Juicy Fruit gum!

Paper dolls and handcrafts kept my attention distracted from my loneliness and impatience with my little brother whom I saw as a nuisance and he often became a victim of my long, pent up unconscious anger. Fantasies and imaginative stories became a valuable escape as I saved and read every movie magazine I could find. I cut out covers and pictures of all those beautiful women, - Betty Grable, Rita Hayworth, Lana Turner - wishing I could be like them, or certainly like my long-held model of perfection, Shirley Temple, who even had a soda bar in her basement! I learned to play the piano during those years and I practiced under the observing eyes and ears of the watchful, impatient grandmother from her "throne" on the couch. Bored with those simplistic songs, I eventually got 35 cents together and went downtown to Heaton's Music store and bought the sheet music for Tommy Dorsey's, *"Boogie Woogie,"* a joyous, exciting, freeing beat I had heard played on the radio next to my bed every morning. Other times I learned to accompany my mother, as her glorious soprano voice sang Gounod's *"Ave Maria."* My love of music, singing, and harmonizing grew from those days, a magical way to escape into another wonderful, carefree world. While in 8th grade, the nuns had me stand on the cafeteria stage and sing to the school assembly, "*I'm a Little Teapot*," complete with appropriate gestures, and then the important new song, "*God Bless America.*"

Eventually, it became obvious that grandma was really unable to tend to Bobbie's and my daily needs, so a "colored girl," Dorothy, was hired to get us off to school, using a curling iron on my very straight hair. She had lunch ready when we walked home for a noon break. In addition, she did meal preparation and general house-cleaning. Grandma mourned from her almost permanent spot on that dark brown velvet, with the radio in the living room corner bringing her the latest war news, interrupted by soap operas.

Today, I reflect on those years and "become" Mary Helen. I am aware of all the Feelings that had been building without relief or appropriate expression ever since Aunt Carmen's pro-nouncement of my father's death. The playground, thankfully, offered many opportunities for physical exercise and social-ization to ease my loneliness. However, six years of repressed emotional energy finally manifested themselves in a physical way when I was 11 years old. Walking down the 13 steps from our upstairs "home" to go to dinner, my legs suddenly collapsed under me and I fell to the bottom landing. Prior leg discomfort had been attributed to "growing pains." This was the begin-ning of what was to be diagnosed as Rheumatic Fever, which then confined me to bed for six weeks, upstairs, and alone, except for my little radio which kept me totally engrossed day after day, from "*Portia Faces Life*" to "*Jack Armstrong, The All-American Boy.*" Again, I escaped into love and adventure. At night, I listened to "*Major Bowes Amateur Hour*," "*Inner Sanctum*," "*Suspense*," and all the wonderful war music which I knew by heart: "*White Cliffs of Dover*," "*I'll Be Seeing You*," The Andrews Sisters, etc...

One of the memorable times that brought me special attention, was a visit by Sister Bertrand and my entire 6th grade class who had walked from school to my house, and each of them brought me a special Get Well letter. Grandma let me sit in bed in grandpa's room so everyone could sit better. Even though I was ill and confined to total bed rest, I felt special, a new awareness. My mother helped me mark that day by buying me a scrapbook, my first "Memory Book," where I could paste all the notes and later add many special mementos from theaters, parties, etc. and write my own comments and dates. Over the years I continued to save special, meaningful things: poems, jokes, and all my own favorites! Somewhere in boxes hidden away under beds, etc., those early scrapbooks remain, stored keepsakes of my launch into the next chapter of my life.

During the following year, I suffered a relapse of the Rheumatic Fever as a result of too much exertion playing tennis in my playground home. I was lucky not to have had any permanent heart damage which is very common among Rheumatic Fever patients. However, as a result, I was not permitted to participate in any Physical Education classes in high school, and until I was 21, I took a daily Sulfadiazine pill as a prophylactic measure.

FEELINGS: (buried) unexpressed but stored: loneliness, guilt, shame, inadequacy, low self-worth, anger, fear of abandonment, needing to look good, be the best, present a façade acceptable to those around me so I could satisfy my basic survival instincts by being what anyone else wanted me to be.

"The most important muse of all is our own inner child." –Stephen Nachmanovitz

Much later in my life when my own first daughter was six years old, I tried to imagine what it had been like for my mother, so suddenly left alone with two small children. I think it was then that I could reflect on how she did her life. How trapped and skin-starved she must have felt, and how she must have felt anger, having to again come under the dominance of her demanding, resentful mother. Looking back, I marvel at what she did to be both parents to Bobbie and me. There were birthday parties and trips to downtown every Saturday for lunch and a movie. Then she let me come to her office at Fort Hayes and meet those important Captains and Colonels in their elaborate uniforms. Because mom had access to the Base Exchange, I was able to purchase cartons of cigarettes (Lucky Strikes) for the most appreciative and handsome red-haired Assistant Pastor, Father Duffy, and then could feel very special as a "chosen one." Although I never achieved the ultimate intimate relationship with my mother (as I have with my own children), I loved and respected her as she struggled against her own mother's control. Grandma had a car, a 1937 Dodge, but allowed no one to use it, even when I was extremely ill with a high fever. Once, because it was raining, she refused to help by going the four blocks to the pharmacy to get my much-needed medication. Our very understanding neighbor answered mom's call for help and drove her to the pharmacy. I don't think my mother ever knew about grandma's emotional and sometimes, physical abuse of my brother and me. We did not want to cause any more troubles for her and grandpa, who did most of the cooking as well, since grandma remained on her self-imposed davenport "throne." However, on Thanksgiving and Christmas, grandma would make a chocolate steamed pudding with a delicious sauce that couldn't be believed. I am proud to have kept that tradition alive in my family and now in theirs.

When it was time for me to go to high school, there were two Catholic Girls' Academies available in Columbus, but the one

I desperately wanted, where all my "fathered" friends were going, was too expensive. My mother did her best to make that happen, and I was able to attain a 50% scholarship so long as I kept my grades high. I was thrilled, and began a four year high school adventure at Saint Mary of the Springs Academy, which was also the Mother House of the Dominican Order of nuns. The school bus picked me up every morning and we rode out to the country location of this high school/ college campus. Those were happy years at last! I did well scholastically, became close friends with seven other girls in particular, and was a Class or Glee Club President every year. I also became fascinated with several well-known authors and/or speakers sponsored by the school "Erskine Lecture Series." It was named for the main class building on campus, and it was a widely attended event. But I became especially fascinated by the words of the then Bishop Fulton J. Sheen, whose piercing eyes and exciting words reached my soul and I would go home and try desperately to share and explain to anyone who would listen about my experience. Grandpa and my mother were usually my best audience.

So many lovely memories of those years, - the chapel and the sounds of the *Gregorian Chant* sung by the Postulants and Novices of the Dominican Order. Another image that comes to mind is that of "The Grotto," set in the rocks which served as the platform for the statue of Mary. And then there was Sister Lauranna, the Directress of the Academy, who was determined to make us all "ladies!" I will never forget Sister Mercia and her sniffing when her errant seniors returned after skipping lunch and driving down to a nearby parking lot for an hour of smoking those forbidden cigarettes, hoping Sen-Sen gum would hide our secrets! To make everyone else proud, I qualified to represent the school by taking the State Exams in Physics my junior year. Then, I received an English Composition medal at graduation in 1949.

However, besides school, I had learned that any extra money I needed would have to be earned, so I took a job at a neighborhood drug store as a "soda jerk," filling myriads of ice cream orders, learning to make change, maintain cleanliness, and present a friendly disposition to all the customers. One evening a very tall, handsome guy in a white uniform (with a massive set of keys attached to his belt), sat at the corner of the counter and enjoyed the fantastic chocolate milk shake - one of my specialties! - I had created for him. After engaging in normal small talk in the otherwise nearly empty store, he asked if he could take me home after work. Of course, I said yes (what did this handsome person see in me?) and he told me his name was "Skip." He was a student at Ohio Wesleyan University and was working as a Psychiatric Aide at the Columbus State Hospital for the Insane! Our first "date" that night included a tour of the grounds of the hospital at midnight before taking me home. Little did I know that was the beginning of a relationship that has lasted to this day, over 60 years!

At this point, I think I should include information about the rest of my "extended family." My mother's sister, Helen, lived with her husband and my three cousins, John, Nancy, and Jeanne in St. Paul, Minnesota. When Uncle John returned from the war, he got married and I now had three new cousins in Columbus: Steve, and the fraternal twins, Francie and Kathie. My father had seven brothers and one sister and we had to leave them and my Swedish grandmother all in Duluth when daddy died. My brother also married and fathered two sons and a daughter, but unfortunately, our families have never been close, and they have no children to add to the cousin-count. Much later, I learned I wasn't the only one with alcohol problems, but in those days, everything was secret. I later learned that my dear cousin John had died of the disease, leaving a wife and four daughters. His mother, Aunt Helen, also became afflicted in later years. But the "no talk" rule was firmly in place in society and as a result, many died from the disease.

My "Memory Book" grew as I savored many special events in those years. After school, many of us would take the city bus downtown in time to go to the late afternoon shows on the stage of the Palace Theater: Glenn Miller, Tommy Dorsey, Vaughn Monroe, and my souvenir autograph of Woody Herman after three of us followed him into the elevator at his nearby hotel. My English teachers, Sister Amata and Sister Francis Gabriel encouraged our reading and saving special poems and stories which we could collect in our own special permanent folders. My mother brought home special articles and jokes from her work which I added to my collection. Many years later I would recall the first stanza of a deeply thought-provoking poem, which for some reason, had a special meaning for me, unknown at the time:

> "I'll give you for a little while, a child of mine,
>
> He said, for you to love and care for, and
>
> mourn for when she's dead" –Anonymous

Although sex education was non-existent in those years, we girls learned what we could by sharing whatever experiences we had or had heard about. I knew that "it" was wrong until you are married, so "heavy petting" seemed to be the only alternative! I dated two other very promising men while dating Skip. Dale was a blonde handsome accounting student at Ohio State, and Ken was a fun dental student. I was closest to Dale and his family (with two parents!), but deep down I knew I felt safer and more attracted to someone as tall as Skip rather than the eye-level height of Dale! Hmm ... What was a little girl looking for? And what was this only son of divorced parents looking for, after leaving his hometown of Lima, Ohio the day after graduation to make his way alone, hoping to find? And how did each of them see their need for each other as their relationship grew, until they became a couple?

> FEELINGS: uncertainty, undercurrent of shame, low self-worth, inadequacy, triumph, dependence, hope, safety, old anger and guilt now almost engraved deeply at the cellular level.

The two years following graduation were difficult. Not having money for college or the Nursing School where many of my friends enrolled, I got a job as a receptionist at a high school on the Ohio State campus and now lived in a rented room away from my family. Grandma had been making my life increasingly more difficult with constant complaining about my late hours on dates with Skip, waking up to the sound of the car in the driveway beneath her window. I became independent of others' constraints, got into and out of scrapes with fellow workers, and deep down, was totally unsettled and alone with myself having no clear parameters for guidance.

"The subconscious works to create the reality according to the programming it has been fed." –Susan Smith Jones

The opportunity to move to St. Paul and live with my Aunt Helen and Uncle Harry and John, Nancy, and Jeanne, looked like a gift from Heaven! So I "ran away" physically this time, looking forward to Skip's promise to visit me. I was successful in getting a job as a Service Representative with the telephone company in downtown St. Paul, and in the meantime, I tried to live within a family structure, which by today's standards would be the role model for dysfunction! At some point I decided maybe I could qualify for a scholarship for a Nursing School in Minneapolis, and was thrilled to be accepted for a full three year term, including uniforms and books.

I had been away from a school setting for two years and suddenly was confronted with massive amounts of memory requirements in Anatomy, Chemistry, and Psychology. I struggled to meet my own standards of high grades, having always to be and look good. I enjoyed the other girls in my class and joined the social events with university students, fraternity parties, etc... I watched others who drank, but that was not in my repertoire of being a "lady." Of course, my cigarettes did well as medicators of any emotional pain I might be experiencing. As studies got more difficult I found myself really lonesome for Skip and the security of our relationship. When I went home for Christmas, we stopped at a jewelry store in downtown Columbus and selected a lovely diamond solitaire engagement ring which we put on lay-away. Skip made monthly payments toward the day I would wear it. He was then a full-time student at Ohio State University, plus he worked at a laboratory at night and at a gas station on weekends.

By the middle of the next school term, my inner inadequacy and fear of failure had reached a crisis point, and knowing I might fail or do less than my expectations, I fabricated an excuse to leave and return home to Columbus "to care for my dear mother" and her increasing problems with her own parents. So I sent a telegram to Skip announcing I was arriving home at 7:00 am Saturday and that I hoped Rogers Jewelry store was missing a ring!

And with that, I have shared with you the first twenty years of my life. To be continued...

With Mother, Ruth Shay and Brother, Bobbie

High School Picture

CHAPTER 2
1951-1971

PART ONE
1951-1961

FEELING

And so it was. I wore the ring and we planned the wedding for September 8th, 1951. I moved back into the upstairs room of my grandparents until that date, meanwhile working as an ad agent for the Columbus newspaper. On a lunch hour one day, I took Skip's monthly payment into the Rogers Jewelry store and was stopped by the owner and offered a job! He had "liked my smile" and wanted someone like me greeting and doing business with his customers! That was a very happy, satisfying time and I stayed there for 20 months when my husband and I, and our daughter, Karen left Columbus for a whole new adventure in the Air Force.

In the meantime, our wedding was a beautiful event and we began our life together. After a honeymoon trip to the Smokey

Mountains, we began our married life in an adorable apartment above a house in a rural community setting nearby, - 1670 Ferris Road - $60.00/month - with fresh tomatoes and corn from our landlord's garden. It was a happy time and it wasn't long before the doctor confirmed my pregnancy and a due date for the following June. There was much excitement, with an unknown challenging future! Skip would graduate with his degree and his commission as a 2nd Lieutenant in the Air Force three weeks before the baby was due and then? Where would we be sent? What would he be doing? They were busy, fun times. I remember once celebrating with a glass of Mogen David wine. Another big memory from those days was the night Skip surprised me with our own brand new television set. Somehow, my "morning sickness that lasted all day" seemed to diminish in intensity after that. I was married two weeks after my 20th birthday and I was a mother two months before my 21st, about to embark on a life two grown-up children couldn't even imagine at that time. But we knew we would be in this together, proven over and over in the 60 years since we said "I do." We left Columbus on my 21st birthday heading for Flight School in Malden, Missouri.

FEELINGS: deep, buried grief and guilt, inadequacy, shame, relief, hope, gratitude along with innocent acceptance.

Malden, Missouri! Where is that? For our first six months in the Air Force, we lived in a little rental house in this tiny town in southeast Missouri. Skip's initial primary flight training took place there and everything about our lives changed. We were away from home and family, familiar surroundings, and we were brand new to our role as parents to this precious baby, Karen Marie. And we were just "children" ourselves. There are no words to describe the awe of motherhood, the realization that this little child was the result of the love of Skip and me, that God is really trusting us to care for this child "He loaned us (remembering that favorite poem from high school)." She was so adorable and became the mascot of other student officers. She would laugh so heartily when one of them would use her as the training plane and fly her around the house, doing rolls, dives, and Immelmanns! Teething and croup were frequent crises to face as a young mom in a strange place. But I look back on those early Air Force years and my heart smiles with happy memories of making new friends from all over the world, and working to find and learn those connecting threads which create lifetime friendships, bonds and shared experiences.

After primary training we went further west, to Vance Air Force Base in Enid, Oklahoma, where Skip was trained as a multi-engine pilot. Despite his preference for jets, the Flight Surgeon explained what would happen to his legs if he ever had to eject from a jet. His 6' 6" height determined his future in multi-engines! In Enid, we rented a lovely little house and I often took Karen to play in the pool at the Officers' Club. Now a year old, Karen was able to do many things with us as we explored the countryside and Base those three months in Enid. At last, Skip earned his Wings to proudly wear on his uniforms.

The next move took us to San Antonio, Texas to Randolph Air Force Base where Skip would be matched up with eight others as a crew for KB 29s. That WW2 bomber had now been converted to tankers in order to conduct air refueling for single engine jets as flying gas stations all over the world!

Having decided that since Karen was so special, we wanted her to have a little sister or brother, I embarked on a new round of morning sickness which wasn't as debilitating as with Karen. So those three months in a "converted chicken coop duplex" were not the most comfortable days. Fortunately, our chicken coop neighbors were also in the same assignment and we all became close friends. Their orders to go to Dow Air Force Base in Maine preceded ours, so fortunately, when we got to Bangor, Maine in mid-February with a temperature of -28°(!), they were able to take us into their rented old New England home, with one central heater in the kitchen!

We all soon moved into a rental housing community, Bangor Garden Homes, which was quickly filled with other Air Force families, members of the Strategic Air Command's 506th Air Refueling Squadron. Their goal was to become combat-ready, and create a Squadron that could operate efficiently and on demand during those Korean/Cold War days. We wives had to learn to be very independent and capable as we could never be sure from where or when our husbands would return from their missions. And those old relic war planes rarely flew without some emergency or engine loss that would keep a crew standing by in air bases around the country, waiting for new parts or engines to be delivered.

So, you see, my life gradually came to have a meaning, all in itself. I could do everything necessary and do it well, looking good, and our friends became the family we had never before known. Karen's baby sister, Kathy Lynn, was born on May 25, 1954, 23 months younger than Karen. Oh, such fun! Two little girls and I got to "play house" for real, not like those imagination-filled days back in grandma's basement! We stayed in Bangor for 18 months and loved the opportunities to visit Bar Harbor, the beaches, and the lobster stands along the roadways. Happily, I discovered that a third child was on the way, and 14 months after Kathy, Kristin Lee joined our family and they were all "the babies" of our many friends, and particularly three bachelor officers living a few houses away; they even came to the Base hospital with Skip and me when I delivered her on July 15th, 1955.

Never having intentionally planned a family of "K" named children, it just seemed so much cuter to not change the pattern already in place! Bangor days were also a very happy chapter in our lives. Our girls were so special, and our friends were our sisters and brothers. We loved the opportunities to travel and adventure to new places, so we weren't too surprised or dismayed to learn our Squadron was to move to Bergstrom Air Force Base in Austin, Texas. So, in August of 1955 (Kris was six weeks old, Kathy, a year, and Karen, three), we loaded ourselves and supplies in our new nine passenger Mercury station wagon, and began our journey south and west, stopping in Lima and Columbus to spend time with grandparents, showing off our three little Roush girls.

FEELINGS: confident, happy, loved, optimistic...but guarded; the inner fear I would be "found out" as a fake, guilty and shamed for something I wasn't even sure of anymore, always a knot tied somewhere deep inside.

Picture this: Driving from Maine to Texas in August with temperatures in the 90's, before air conditioning. We carried our few possessions on the roof rack; we had two little girls and a six week old baby playing and sleeping on the crib mattress behind us, and foil-covered windows to try to deflect the sun, mile after mile, motel after motel. Amazing, now when I think of it, but at that time we just did what we had to do and enjoyed the adventure.

A highlight (?) of that trip took place as we drove south through Missouri, past Fort Leonard Wood, and baby Kris was due for a bottle but the car bottle warmer wouldn't work! Those were the days when everything had to be sterile, with excessive care in preparing formulas and bottles. I had an electric bottle warmer set up in each motel room to prepare the next day's bottles. I had only one bottle left for that day, and it was cool in our ice chest, so

I suggested we stop at a restaurant and ask if they would please warm the bottle for me like I would do – standing in a pan of heating water. Imagine my surprise and shock when the waitress poured the milk from the bottle into a pan, heated it, and poured it back into the bottle, even using her fingers to replace the nipple cap! I was horrified, in shock and fear, knowing that Kris's cries of hunger were getting louder every minute. Fearing the irreparable damage I was probably doing to this precious baby, I had no choice but to allow her to ingest this tainted, carefully crafted formula as I asked God to keep her safe and not punish me for not having a back-up bottle for any such emergency as this! I was consumed by guilt, shame, and deep gratitude when no adverse effects were apparent. But that is one of those memory-making incidents that still is as real as if it was yesterday!

Eventually arriving in Austin, we learned we couldn't get on-Base housing right away, so we had to rent a little unfurnished house which was down the embankment from the taxiway of the Austin airport. Our furniture would not arrive for another two weeks, so we had to "make do" with borrowed cots from the base, a card table and two folding chairs, with the crib mattress surrounded by suitcases. Kris had her own car bed. On our way through Columbus we had bought a stove and refrigerator but they also would not arrive at the Base for another two weeks. Visiting Skip's dad and his wife in Lima, Mary gave us a deep fat fryer, so that became our stove and I could heat bottles there. Foods were kept cold in two ice chests which Skip would have to replenish at least twice a day due to the stifling heat of the Texas summer. Using a laundromat to wash diapers, I would bring them home to hang and dry on the back yard clothes lines, and look up to hear and see the wingtips of taxiing airplanes passing by on their way to the runway. Around my feet I felt, saw, and heard those quick, slithering lizards making their way through the dry brush, otherwise known as grass when there was enough rain.

Somehow, we survived this "adventure" without much mishap, and were notified that a unit on the Base was available to us, so we joyfully were re-united with our own furniture, linens and dishes and marveled to finally have our very own stove and refrigerator! So we joined the Base housing community and again were part of another family of loving, caring, empathetic wives of husbands again involved with setting up their Air Refueling Squadron at this Base. As wives, we were taught how important we were to the success of the squadron's "mission," and how necessary it was for us to see that our husbands remained emotionally stable and reassured of our ability to manage our homes and families if and when they would fly off on up to 12- hour missions. Again, they were frequently delayed in other places due to parts failures. Of course, SAC would frequently pull "Alerts," practice evacuations for families and specific requirements for crews to be airborne in a matter of minutes. All the wives were members of SAC's "Dependents Assistance Program," and part of committees which would gear into instant action especially in the event of an air casualty. Then, the Chaplain, Commanding Officer, and a committee wife would call on the now-classified "widow" to inform her, and then go into action with other women to help her in every conceivable way with family notices, children, food, funeral planning, etc... Others of us became Red Cross "Grey Ladies," volunteering for any and all possible hospital duties.

Naturally, in case of an "Alert," we had our instructions on how to evacuate women and children and we were timed on this evacuation execution. One of those times, we formed our procession of station wagon car pools, each one filled with children, water, food, toys, etc. and drove off to the nearby Bastrop State Park where we spent the day fighting heat and mosquitoes until the "All Clear" was sounded and we were free to leave. As it turned out, mine was the first car to lead the procession out of the park on a narrow dirt road. It wasn't long before I realized I had a flat tire! No one could move until our car was cleared. I laugh now when I remember how quickly our accompanying airmen got that tire changed and we all could be on our way home. Ah, memories and motor scooters!

FEELINGS: happy, a sense of belonging, excited, anticipatory, proud, assured, but deep down, a lingering doubt and shame: "Do I deserve this?"

Living on Base was a fun adventure in itself. Skip could get to the Flight Line quickly with his new, red Cushman motor scooter, so I would have the car for my errands, etc... By then, Karen was four years old and she delighted in standing in front of her daddy on the scooter and cruising through the streets of the Base housing project, her white-blonde hair blowing in the wind and her squeals of delight that would herald their arrival. Kathy was two then, and after many appointments with her pediatrician to explain her apparent discomfort and sad mood, it was decided to remove her adenoids which had resulted in chronic ear pain, frequently infected. I was so upset that we hadn't known earlier, especially when she exhibited a new happy personality, now pain-free. She and Karen had many young friends to play with; at one time, trying to produce new hairstyles, they had a great time with scissors on each other's hair with near-disastrous results! Baby Kris was such a good girl and would love to sit and bounce in her special swing as she watched her older sisters and their play.

Those last 18 months of Air Force life were truly the best and we made friends with whom we relate to this day. The shared experience and history of the Air Force families and all the stress we learned to live with, created a bond that even now produces an "instant intimacy" as if those days were last week. Skip's Air Refueling Squadron remained combat-ready and they flew regularly scheduled 12-plus hour missions meeting and refueling those gas-hungry F84-F jets all over the world. The squadron spent three months TDY (temporary duty) in Anchorage, Alaska over the winter and came back with a variety of stories of incidents trying their best to maintain his aircraft in way-below zero temperatures. The wives and children stayed on the Base; many left to visit families, but we had created our own "family" and never felt alone. Someone was always "there."

It was during that period in Austin that Skip began to question his future with the Air Force – or not. With all the moving, motels, and restaurants we had experienced over those last four years, and particularly a favorite dining place we found in Austin, "The Terrace Motel," Skip had been observing the variety of management operations in the hospitality business. The idea of leaving the Air Force after his time was over began to percolate into thoughts that he could easily learn that business and do a better job than what he had been experiencing. The last six months at Bergstrom were spent in deep reflection, conversation, and torn loyalties. He had come to really love to fly, but the idea of being a civilian commercial airline pilot just didn't "fit" the flying roles he enjoyed; at least if he ever "augered in" (crashed) with SAC, it would have been for a greater purpose than that of an airline taxi driver! Skip saw the military as a no-win, too regimented future with no real opportunity for advancement based on merit rather than years. In the meantime, he visited the offices of the Texas Restaurant Association in Austin and learned more about education, business requirements and opportunities. They even offered him a scholarship to remain and train in Austin and pursue a career in Texas.

Meanwhile, I had my own struggles coming to grips with the idea of losing this family and going back to being a "civilian!" To add to the conflict, one day when Skip was out flying, the Commanding

Officer and the Chief Operations Officer knocked on my door and talked to me about how to urge my husband to stay with the Squadron as they really valued his performance. But that was not to be.

In September, 1958, we drove out the gate of Bergstrom for the last time and began our trip back to Columbus, where Skip would re-enroll at Ohio State to get his additional education requirements necessary for a hotel/restaurant career. It wasn't until we travelled less than 20 miles that I felt a very deep tension in my body start to loosen and I realized how unconsciously I had been prepared in case one day the Chaplain appeared at my door. And now, in its place, was the awareness of another pregnancy's early term, thus knowing we would have to be "settled" in our new strange life before February, 1959.

FEELINGS: fear, grief, resentment, uncertainty, sad, lonely, resigned, doubtful...coupled with morning sickness

I remember trying to be calm and "matter of fact" about life and its changes, trying to reassure my precious little girls about the loss of their home and friends, trying to get them excited at the prospect of seeing their grandmas and grandpas in Ohio again. And, I tried to convince myself of the same realities. I knew Skip was full of his own feelings as well, but I don't remember our ever sharing them with each other. It was just "life;" deal with it! I can only imagine his own fears and responsibilities as he gave up what he knew, loved, and excelled at. Now his future was a big question mark and he had a wife and four children to consider.

Back in Ohio, we set about searching for a place to live and fortunately, found a three bedroom home on a quiet street in Gahanna, a suburb of Columbus. What would have been an attached garage had been converted to a playroom right off the kitchen - an ideal set up for the girls with their ever-increasing numbers of dolls, books, riding horse, and games. They were happy to make new friends immediately with the children next door and down the street. A backyard pool provided much splashing for everyone the following summer.

In the meantime, Skip bought a second car, a little Morris Minor, so he could get to his classes and then to work for a well-known Columbus restaurateur, "Stew" Harrison, on the other side of town. There, he had the opportunity to learn the very basics of restaurant operation and dining room management. Of course, those were the hours when others went out to eat, so we learned to live without him for hours at a time as his schedule was so hectic and full.

We made it through the holidays, and my fourth child would soon be with us. By then I was discouraged, sad, and lonely, despite being back in my home city. The SAC planes from nearby Lockbourne Air Force Base flew their patterns over our house and I longed for the security and old life we had been given. Nearby, my mother was still working at her Civil Service job, and Skip's mother and step-father (Max), were active members of their Masonic communities. Grandma could no longer be left alone as she slipped into dementia, and her full-time companion, Dollie, became a beloved member of the family. Grandpa still maintained his floor of leather goods at Smith Brothers Hardware Company, an old, established firm that is still doing business at the same Columbus location. On a recent visit to Columbus, I was shocked to see the building again, and many memories flooded back in my mind.

On February 20th, our beautiful daughter, Kimberly Sue ("deedoo, deedoo," as Grandpa Max would tease her) was born at the same hospital and with the same OB who had delivered Karen seven years earlier. The fact that I was running a fever and had some kind of infection made it necessary for me to remain in the hospital an extra day. That really created a disturbance in Skip's work schedules and his mother's plans to care for the other girls while I was gone! I was so excited to bring Kimberly home for all her sisters to meet, but within an hour of my return, Skip had to go back to work and his mother had to keep a previous hair appointment, but she explained that she had taken a round steak out of the freezer to thaw so I could pound it out and have Swiss steak for dinner. And there I was, alone again, with my four little girls who needed me!

That day/event has lived in my memory these many years and I can still recall my Feelings of *fear, wrapped around my happiness, and tinged with anger at abandonment*, but determined as always, "I can do it...I'll show you!" And so I did.

The weeks that followed brought more depression and anguish each time I heard and saw those planes. Even Skip was exhausted and discouraged and, after much discussion, agreed to re-apply for Air Force active duty. After waiting awhile to be sure, the envelope was mailed and we waited.

It was during that time that Skip was approached by the owners of a well-known restaurant chain in Ohio and Michigan, and offered a job at their downtown Columbus restaurant with the understanding that in September, they would move us to suburban Detroit where he would be the opening General Manager of their deluxe new Greenfield's Cafeteria in the affluent community of Birmingham, north of Detroit. This offer was just the chance he had been waiting for and his excitement, plus the prospects for a whole new adventure took precedence over our earlier decision to return to the Air Force. He immediately wrote a letter to the Air Force, rescinding his earlier application but we had no idea if it was too late. As fate would have it, over the Memorial Day weekend, his orders and letter had crossed in the mail, and our orders to report to Homestead Air Force Base, Florida in September were thereby withdrawn!

And so it was, we drove away from our Gahanna house with Kathy looking through the back window saying that "our house will be lonesome!" In August, 1957, we moved into our rented two story home in Royal Oak, Michigan, and prepared Karen to start Kindergarten.

FEELINGS: awe-struck, doubtful, hopeful, sad, excited, afraid, unsure of myself (but wouldn't show it), proud, uncertain, and inadequate

NOTE: I am aware that as my writing of this book approached the move to Detroit, Feelings of "unsettlement" and sadness seemed to be trying to manifest themselves, and perhaps it is due to the awareness that in the six to seven years to come, those earlier seeds of doubt, guilt, inadequacy, and fear would make themselves known in what was to be a destructive path my life would travel.

"There is pain in change and there is pain in staying the same. Pick the one that moves you forward" –Motto of the Private Practice of Kristin L. Roush, Ph.D.

All the excitement of daddy's new life experience and the opportunities to grow and learn new things in new places were the themes that permeated our thoughts and reassurances to our four precious little girls. Our corner house in Royal Oak had a fenced back yard to assure safety for the girls' play equipment and increasing energy! There were two bedrooms downstairs and a great dormer room upstairs where Karen and Kathy could share their own space. Kris and Kim were growing fast and it wasn't long before Kim began to walk. She felt safe walking between people or furniture she could hold onto, but one day she reached under the kitchen sink for the bottle of Joy dish detergent, held on to it with both hands, and took her first solo steps across the room to Krissy, who was coaxing her toward her! To this day, I still often refer to "Krissy" instead of Kris!

One of the big blessings of that house was the Babiarz (baby-ars) family who lived to the back of our fence, most particularly, Alan Babiarz, Karen's age. They became great friends, both sharing their love of ball-playing and sports. The entire Babiarz family became dear friends of us all, as did a couple across the street, also with two young children. Days were full and busy, and for me, lonely. Skip was away most of the time, preparing for the opening of his lovely new restaurant. And of course, he had to quickly get to meet and know his superiors as well as those who would soon be calling him "Manager." One time, he took us all to see the nearly finished building with its beautiful décor, and its prominent place in the very center of the affluent Birmingham suburb, just north of Royal Oak.

As I so clearly remember, and must comment about, the old piano from my Columbus home was ensconced in our living room, and it provided hours and hours of fun and enjoyment teaching the girls my favorite songs from my childhood: "Little Man You've Had a Busy Day," "This Little Piggy Went to Market," "Polly Wolly Doodle," "I'm a Little Teapot," etc... Music continued to be a major part of my life even then, and I eventually joined a community chorus and sang harmony in many classical pieces, "*The Messiah*" being the very special one!

I will never forget my Feelings the day I sent Karen off down the sidewalk, with Alan, to her first day of Kindergarten just a block away. She was wearing her red and white print dress, her blonde pony tails flying, as she excitedly bounced away. I suddenly realized I would no longer have "control" over her life experiences, nor be with her as she encountered new people and unfamiliar situations. It was a sobering thought and I recalled it in later years as each of the children took those first tentative steps into "the unknown." I thought about my mother, losing her husband when Bobbie and I were so young. So, at least I could console myself that I really wasn't totally alone, despite the long days and nights filled with the talk and laughter shared with my wonderful foursome.

One day, answering a knock at the door, I met a man selling life insurance. I was apparently so impressed by being able to carry on an intelligent conversation with an adult - about adult matters, - I signed us up for a Prudential Life Insurance Policy! At a later time, Skip recalled having had a dream that he came home from work one day, only to find me sitting on the floor playing with the kids, but only able to talk "baby talk!" So near true!

I loved being the efficient housewife, like all the magazines and the TV professed! I baked, cleaned, and used my little green sewing machine to make curtains. I poured over decorating books for fancy new (inexpensive) ideas so I could try to show off the perfection of my role as wife and mother. I was stalwart and strong in medical emergencies and other crises that occurred. My adrenaline knew to kick in and produce this "Master Mom" who could handle the world. I worked hard at it, I think partly to prove to myself that I could be a good wife, even to a "civilian" who was overseeing peoples' eating habits rather than flying in glory for the good of all the world! Hmm.....

Naturally, Christmases were the big time to shine, and we did it up well, with visits from Santa Claus, grandparents, and friends. Of course, dinners were complete with all the trappings of traditional fare. And then the news: a new baby was on the way! By then, I had really come to know that after four babies, it didn't make much difference in numbers and I was truly excited to have a new baby for all of us to love! Naturally, there were many jokes about whether a boy would be possible, and friends took bets, a fun adventure for us all. What a shock it was when, on March 18, 1959, our ten pound, two ounce son, Michael Joseph was born! Skip was in such shock as he left the hospital that he tells of letting the door slam on his fingers that night. And yes, we decided to break the cycle of "Ks" if this young boy dared to take on the task of having four older sisters. So "Mike" was the strongest and most masculine name we could pick and he has turned out to live up to that early naming decision.

Naturally, the girls were so excited that they would have a baby brother and they all gathered around as I laid him on our bed to change his first diaper at home. The girls had no idea what genital differences there might be, but as soon as he was exposed and relieved himself, the girls cried out "He squirt the ceiling, mommy!" And so another chapter began.

At some time prior to Michael's birth, my super-woman image began to crack a bit when I was having difficulty breathing enough air in my lungs, so, of course, I needed to see a doctor who was concerned that I might have Pleurisy. After examining me and finding no further evidence, he began to question me about my life, experiences, and activities. What seemed normal and natural to me by then, apparently signaled some different thoughts in him and he proceeded to educate me about some of the latest medical findings in the 1950s about a condition called "Stress," and how it can often manifest itself in sometimes severe physical symptoms. But ah, the good news was that new medications had been developed and were designed to relieve those unknown inner anxieties of "Stress," thereby relieving those outward symptoms. He very happily and optimistically prescribed a newer medication called Equanil, which should surely be the answer to my problems. Naturally, you do what the doctor says, and I began what was to become a dependence on this type of miraculous elixir, which truly did relieve my breathing symptoms, and I could feel whole and energized again.

FEELINGS: out of control, therefore a controller on the outside...inadequate, therefore becoming a perfectionist on the outside...low self-worth, manifesting a super-woman image to the world...plus the old guilt and shame...unworthy.

> "Do not fear mistakes. There are none."
> –Miles Davis

Slowly, almost imperceptibly, Skip's and my relationship became more and more distant. He was rarely at home and when he did spend time there, the children demanded his willing attention until, exhausted, he would retreat to bed to be ready to start another 18 hour day, holidays and weekends included. There were, however, rare times when we joined our neighbors across the street after the kids were asleep, and helped each other try to learn to play Bridge. Karen guarded the house and watched TV while the little ones slept, but she could signal us by blinking the porch light, which we could easily see from our card table. One night, the light blinked and we raced over, only to have her tell us, "Nothing's wrong; I just wanted to see if this would work!"

I had to find and create my own social life by then, and so I became a member of the South Oakland County Newcomers' Club, with a membership of over 100 women, all new to the area just like us. I enjoyed their many activities and decided it was time for me to learn this Bridge game thing that seemed to occupy so much time and fun for other women - mothers just like me - and we all had babysitters to help assure at least one afternoon a week out of the house. Occasionally, I took the children to "daddy's restaurant" for dinner, and we watched him work, although he could never join us and actually sit down.

I guess like other romantic women, I eagerly anticipated our upcoming 10th wedding anniversary, September 8th, 1961, and hoped Skip would remember and we would do something special...just us. Meantime, he had been promoted to become the Manager of the busiest of the company's restaurants in downtown Detroit, serving hundreds of people each day. I will always remember, and can picture myself, celebrating alone at his restaurant, sitting at a corner counter stool, eating a piece of apple pie with a cup of coffee, as he busily juggled his duties between the restaurant's two floors full of hungry demanding customers.

FEELINGS: anger, resentment, loss, grief, abandoned, rejected, lonely, frustrated, hopeless

"It always comes back to the same necessity... go deep enough and there is a bedrock of truth, however hard" –May Sarton

By then, we had been in Detroit for four years and our growing family felt stretched at the seams in our little house. After much searching and deliberation, and the loving support of a gracious real estate lady, we were able to buy our very first house, four miles further south in Berkley, just two blocks from Detroit's main thoroughfare, Woodward Avenue. This old brick house with an extra-large fenced lot with garage, and close to schools, was the answer to a dream! Somehow, we found a mortgage payment we could afford, to meet the $15,900 selling price. Being a new homeowner with all the necessary "fix up" projects awaiting my skillful, imaginative attention, I proceeded to no longer rely on my husband to fill my loneliness. I had so many fun things to create and enjoy!

The second floor of 1441 Catalpa was a huge dormer-type room, and all four girls could share their own space, while one year-old Michael stayed in his crib in his room next to ours. I converted the third downstairs bedroom into a den, where the old piano from my childhood found its home, across from a comfy day bed, tables, and my tiny indispensable white FM radio (which played lovely music all the time). I had books and magazines, a "retreat" all my own! The piano had become an integral part of our family's furniture, and I took great delight in continuing to play all that children's music from my childhood, and we added several more to our repertoire! Occasionally, we invited couples from our Newcomer's family over to our house for sing-along parties. Alcohol was never an issue in our lives. I had never seen or known about it in my childhood, although I do remember at certain holiday times when grandma wasn't around, grandpa would reach behind the corner cookie jar in the kitchen, call for my mother, and he'd mix something like "Four Roses" with some ginger ale, which they enjoyed together over the breakfast room table. And I remember once in the Air Force, Skip learned to enjoy "Rhine Wine" with a spaghetti dinner, and he couldn't wait to teach me how to sip and taste this magic elixir before swallowing on top of the marinara sauce! At Officers' Wives Club luncheons, we'd be served a small glass of wine with our salads. When we played Bridge with the neighbors, we shared a half gallon of beer among the four of us, to wash down the crackers and the snacks. And, I guess we provided beer and mixes when we entertained. Skip took care of that and I had no interest in drinking or not.

However, one Sunday afternoon, we were invited to an afternoon get-together at the home of a very "proper" couple from Scotland, plus several of our other Newcomers' friends. Skip remembered a punch recipe one of his crewmen had introduced to the others during their Alaska deployment. Eleanor readily accepted the recipe for "Banyon Tree Punch," which consisted of a bottle of vodka, a bottle of gin, one large can of pineapple juice, a jar of honey, and lots and lots of ice. I "sipped along" with everyone else and had a very good time. We all had a great laugh as Eleanor fell, face-first into a bush near their front door. But what I really recall is the difficulty I had navigating up the steps to our house, where I slept it off. That was such a horrid experience, I knew I would never again get myself into such a situation, and I didn't (Well...?).

Meanwhile, the girls had started school, and poor Kris was so frightened the first day, I had a terrible time finally having to leave her with the reassurance that I would be there to pick her up each day! The girls had great times together and loved their big sand box and swing set in our great fenced yard. They shared such a variety of interests, from dolls to cowboy play. Karen was so thrilled to learn that a member of the Detroit Pistons basketball team lived right next door! Kim would dress up in her cowboy outfit including hat and boots, pretend a broom was a microphone, and stand on the front porch singing to any passers-by, "I eat all my crust! I eat all my crust!" They all loved their baby brother and we enjoyed great laughs and photos as Mike's hand scooped up hunks of his first birthday chocolate cake!

Skip's mother knew I had my trusty little sewing machine. She once came to visit, bringing several yards of a most beautiful mauve brocade material. I had never attempted anything so challenging, but I considered this to be a new challenge, so I bought a pattern for a sheath dress with full zipper up the back, plus enough wine velvet material to make a bolero jacket to wear with it. I also decided to line both pieces and make a two inch wide belt of the same mauve material! What a task I'd set for myself, but with some coaching from a seamstress who lived nearby, I finally completed that beautiful outfit and I can't count the number of times I had to rip out and re-set that zipper! I have carried it with us through every move since then, and much later used my "creation" as part of a paper I wrote, as a metaphor trying to prove that I contained love within me just as God created me with His special love. But that is part of my life to come. NOTE: Recently, I lost quite a bit of weight due to some medical problems, and dared to try on the dress again! With some zipper effort, I wore it long enough for Skip to take a picture I could send to the family, and then removed it in order to breathe again.

All the while, Skip continued to excel in his management role and was highly praised by his superiors as well as his employees and customers. He learned every aspect of food service, meeting and solving myriads of emergencies that could occur in such a busy operation. However, Skip's job duties kept him away most of the time and he worked hard at becoming successful, all the while being responsible for the house and five young children. So, I took a more active role in the large Newcomers' Club. I made new friends and even became President. Skip and I were rarely able to socialize as a couple due to his schedule, and gradually we seemed to drift further apart.

Because of the high performance standards he had set for himself, Skip had been observed by some executives of a company called "Hot Shoppes," who owned several restaurants in Washington, DC, plus four hotels, two in DC, one in Dallas, and one in Philadelphia. They invited both of us to come to the annual National Restaurant Association convention in Chicago, where we would meet several of them at the Palmer House. It was an exciting time, and it was followed by an invitation to attend the annual Management Picnic to be held at J.W. Marriott's - the company's founder - Fairfield Farm in the Virginia countryside. It was a spectacular event and we met and enjoyed everyone there. As a result, Skip was offered a job and a move to DC where he would go into training, learning about their restaurant standards and organization. There was no doubt that this would be his proper direction and we quickly made flight arrangements for him to move and get acquainted with the area and maybe find us a house. In the meantime, I stayed in Detroit to hopefully sell our house by myself. We couldn't afford a realtor's charges, although our kind, original real estate woman offered to help me with the legal forms. That was a strange, unsettling time. Skip and I had grown much more emotionally distant, and when I drove him to the airport for his flight to DC, he was angry and not sure if he even wanted us to move to DC with him.

FEELINGS: anger, lonely, abandoned, fear, guilty, uncertain...low self-worth

That was the autumn of 1961, and I set about preparing the house to look inviting to any prospective buyers. That meant painting all the walls of the concrete block basement! Each night after the kiddies were in bed, I'd return to the basement, completing that job. More often than not, I used tooth brushes to get into all the tiny little porous cracks of the concrete! And my trusted little white radio would keep me company with its calming, lovely background music.

Skip's letters began to sound more positive and he was very excited about what he was learning and the other men he was meeting. When I was finished with the painting, I sat at the kitchen counter and wrote him about what was happening with the house sale efforts, made more difficult due to the recession Detroit was enduring at that time. One day, a beautiful German Shepherd dog jumped our fence and came to play with the girls and he adopted us! He had no tags and there were no responses to my "Found" ad or reports of a missing dog with the Animal Shelters. So, besides the house selling, five children, another dog ("Shaggy" had already come to live with us through Karen's school teacher whose dog had had pups), painting the basement walls, and trying to retain Newcomers' Club friends, it was a frustrating, stressful autumn. But, of course, I was still taking those pills the doctor had prescribed for me, so at least I wasn't suffering those old Pleurisy symptoms.

During one of those long dreary weekends, a couple we knew from Newcomers decided I needed a break, so I got a baby sitter and went with them as their guest to the well-known "Fox and Hounds" restaurant for a steak dinner. Oh, I was so relieved to be "out" a bit. Before dinner, as was their custom, drinks were to be ordered and I had no idea what to order, so they introduced me to a martini. To this day I refer to that drink as the "beginning of the end." Right after about the second sip went down, I experienced a total transformation of my inner being! It was as if a knot I had had deep inside, unknown, was suddenly gone and I only knew it by its absence...as I had never been aware of the knot...or as they say, "the hole in my soul."

> FEELINGS: relief, joy, relaxation, self-assurance, freedom, happy, wonder, amazement...a new medication for those years of buried feelings

Of course, now I can realize I had also been faithfully taking my benzodiazepine, Equanil, something that should never be combined with alcohol, so I was getting as much as four times the effect of the alcohol. But, in those early tranquilizer years, the medical profession had not yet learned that.

Suddenly, my life seemed to take on a new meaning, and after inquiring about the ingredients in that drink, I determined I could fix it at home and enjoy that warmth as I listened to my music and wrote long letters to Skip each night. And so it all began. When Skip made a surprise visit back home one weekend, we both enjoyed those martini-soaked olives! At one time we even had a travel case with a shaker, to make those "wonderful drinks" when we travelled anywhere! We both recognized the ease with which we were able to "communicate" after a few sips. Neither of us experienced any craving, only a social lubricant!

At last, the house sold, the German Shepherd went for training as a seeing-eye dog, Skip found a great house for us in Arlington, Virginia, and we left Detroit to start our new life in the East. We arrived at our new home just one week before Christmas, 1961, and my mother was to arrive to celebrate her December 23rd birthday and spend the holidays with us at our new home.

Being the perfectionist I had become, we were totally unpacked, moved in, Christmas tree and decorations up before mom arrived. Our house was lovely; the Catholic school was nearby and there were wonderful hills where the kids could join the neighbor children to sled and enjoy the winter snows. Skip, by now, had completed his training and requested a move to the Hotel Division of the company which would eventually become known as the Marriott Corporation. We all came under the spell of "The District...the center of the world," and we went sight-seeing every chance we could get. Of course, the Washington Monument is visible from any direction, so when we went to the top to look at the 360° views, Michael suddenly began to cry, "But where's the Washington Monument?" Another time, after circling the statue of Abraham Lincoln at the Memorial and preparing to move on, we discovered Michael had lost his shoe, at the top of all of those steps!

It was a happy time. I quickly joined the Arlington Chapter of Sweet Adelines to learn more about and enjoy this barbershop style, a cappella harmony. I had been exposed to it just prior to our move when a quartet from the local chapter came to perform for one of our Newcomers' programs. I was stunned to realize that I had never even heard of this group's existence, who met not far from my house. Instead, I had been feeding my music bug with heavy-duty types of accompanied music. The women assured me I would find a similar chapter in DC, and I excitedly became a member and was "hooked" on this singing style - without reading notes from a book - lasting to this day! After weekly rehearsals, we stopped at a nearby tavern for sandwiches and singing. I only drank Coke and apparently didn't "need" the old fortifier as much. However, the new family doctor I met in Arlington decided the newest and more effective stress-relief drug, Librium, should replace my Equanil. I guess it must have been obvious that I was stressed, with all these children, changes, and losses.

And then...I was pregnant again! A new Roush would join us in early December. So again, I was donned in maternity clothes, and we all looked forward to a next Christmas with six little children.

We had made new friends through Skip's work and my Sweet Adeline sisters. Skip was given many opportunities to attend government-sponsored functions, and we learned and enjoyed all the facets of the DC social circuit. John Kennedy was President then, and our girls were thrilled to see Jackie and her children coming to daddy's hotel to enjoy their ice skating rink.

> "Nobody objects to a woman being a good writer or sculptor or geneticist if at the same time she manages to be a good wife, good mother, good-looking, good-tempered, well groomed, and unaggressive." –Leslie McIntyre

Occasionally, during the months that followed, I would find myself wanting that old martini Feeling, and began to occasionally fix myself a drink, sit out on our screened porch among the trees, listen to music, and feel at peace with the world. However, I began to be concerned about my <u>wanting </u>to drink. I knew that was not the way a lady behaved, so I discussed it with my doctor, who decided if I took more of the Librium (!), I'd have no need to use alcohol to achieve that inner glow. One of the special things that happened was our purchase of some new furniture, including a beautiful radio/stereo system, and music became our constant companion as we purchased more LPs and established a lovely record collection we could store in our new Ethan Allen (!) cabinet that matched the stereo! We still had my ancient piano, which found its place down in the basement playroom. The girls became involved with school and scout activities, and Skip was recognized as a successful Food and Beverage Manager in the Marriott system.

FEELINGS: satisfied, controlling, inner uncertainty and inadequacy (hidden perfectionism), lonely, worried about Skip...seeming distant again...and always working holidays and weekends.

September 8, 1951

Skip, Air Force Pilot (1953)

Visiting Grandma Shay on the way to Austin, TX (1955)

CHAPTER 2
1951-1971

PART TWO
1962-1971

FEELING, DEALING

Two months before the baby's due date, I was suffering from a very bad cold and a hacking cough. I noticed a little discoloration and tenderness on my ever-increasing abdomen, and made a special appointment to see my OB the evening of October 1st. He surmised that I probably just bumped the edge of a table, and would be OK. Baby and heart sounds were normal and I was, by then, quite familiar with those feelings of carrying around a new life and all the discomfort now would be quickly forgotten after childbirth.

The following day, October 2, 1962, my coughing continued and by 11:00 am, I knew something was wrong. I called my husband at work and he rushed home. My primary care doctor actually came to my home, and called 911. I remember calling my friend, Shirley, to come and take care of my children when they came home from school. My next memory is of sirens, then being wheeled through corridors at Georgetown Hospital, seeing the ceiling whizzing by. I asked to see a priest, but they assured me that one had already been called. From all the symptoms, the doctors assumed that the uterus had ruptured, and I would require an emergency Caesarian to save the baby. However, as it turned out, the uterus was in place, but the primary, epigastric artery on the right side of my abdomen had ruptured and I had a hematoma "the size of a football." In the recovery room, I remember hearing the doctor telling Skip, "She's not out of the woods yet," and I was aware I was leaving it all behind and was going somewhere amazingly calm and peaceful...and I let go. Suddenly, the sound of Skip's sobbing as he stood over me, created a thought, "He really does care and my family needs me" and I began to return to the room. A nurse who had kept her stethoscope moving over my abdomen suddenly called out, "I feel a heartbeat!" The baby had survived. Having been schooled in Catholic principles and church laws, I remembered that in such a case as this, if it's a question to save the child or the mother, the child is the priority. And I was in a Catholic hospital. I believe that God directed me to come back from that near-death experience in order to resume my maternal duties and ultimately work to complete the task of finding my own life's purpose. It was also, eventually, one of the factors that influenced my later distancing of myself from the Church.

The next two months were a series of set-backs and feelings of doubt, fear, and helplessness. After two weeks in the hospital, and a room festooned with a myriad of flowers and notes from Mr. Marriott, plus all my Sweet Adeline friends, I returned home.

Before 48 hours had passed, my incision ruptured and at 3:00 am, another ambulance rushed me back to Georgetown. The children woke up to have mommy gone again. This time, with the baby doubling its weight in those last two months, the doctor used wire staples to lace me up and hold everything together! While watching the leaves change color as I looked out my hospital window, I became aware of the "Cuban Missile Crisis" taking place out in the world, and my children in school were instructed to take blankets and bottles of water with them to school. I listened to the helicopters helping the evacuation of our country's top officials. One of my nurses/nuns assured me she placed notes of prayers in the pew of the nearby church where President and Mrs. Kennedy went to daily mass. During all this time, I was overcoming infections with tetracycline and unremitting pain was relieved with heavy doses of narcotics, until my body looked like a pin cushion, having injections of Dilaudid given to me in my legs. I remember becoming aware of the soothing effects of those drugs and I developed a high tolerance, requiring increasing doses of a myriad of drugs.

After two more weeks in the hospital, I returned home, 28 pounds lighter, confined to bed, and not allowed to sit up more than a 30° angle to prevent any pressure on the staples. The official due date was a month away, December 2nd. Naturally, there were fears of how a normal vaginal delivery could affect my vulnerable abdominal wounds. Meanwhile, J.W. Marriott and his executive committee assumed all of the mounting financial obligations involved and again filled my room with flowers. They also saw to it that a housekeeper would be hired to oversee all the household and child-care duties. My little daughters did everything they could to minister to me and I did share with them the worrisome possibility that our new baby might have suffered oxygen deprivation. We prayed that would not be so. The wires were finally removed and I was encouraged to walk as much as I could to regain strength and stamina to facilitate a normal delivery. The miracle that resulted after all this trauma was that our sixth child, Kay Therese, was born on her due date, and was perfect in every way possible. Ultimately, it was learned that the particular antibiotic I had taken would likely have an effect on her first set of teeth, which had a tinge of yellow. There is no way I can describe my Feelings after that birth, as I laid in my bed late that night in wonderment and thankful prayers, reflecting on all that had happened in that two month period of trauma.

> "Spiritual growth is about confronting fear in order to attain wonderment." –Jane Nakken

Christmas of 1962 was a time of relieved celebration as the children welcomed their new baby sister to the family. During the night feeding times, I wrote a long epic poem to my obstetrician, "Smiling Jack Sanders," describing the entire two month's story and his ready responses!

The Saga of Smiling Jack Sanders
(or)
"A Stitch in Time Saves Nine (Months)"

'Twas not so very long ago, a certain doctor that we know

Was called upon to do his best

And put his judgment to a test.

Together with his able team,

He found the cause and sewed a seam.

For what had been a mystery, was new to Georgetown history.

Alas, his troubles didn't end;

His needlework refused to mend!

The patient called so late one night,

Announcing, "Doc, things don't look right!"

What to do with this incision?

Soon he made the big decision.

He laced his patient up with wires and clamped them shut with handy pliers.

But then his problems really doubled; he found his patient always troubled.

Besides her moans and aches and wails,

Her mother fretted and chewed her nails.

He finally sent her home at last; she hope that she's recover fast.

She lay in bed in desperation, fighting constant constipation!

For four weeks she almost left him alone (except for some tears on the telephone).

His patient's patience soon wore thin. He must have thought,

"I just can't win!"

Then came the day she'd faced with dread

As she laid, writing in her bed.

The giant staples now must go...she'd have their pulling ache no mo' (!)

Doctor arrived with tool kit handy, cut the wires and all was dandy.

She kept repeating all the while, "It only hurts when I smile."

The next three weeks she'd have to scurry. Baby's here in a hurry.

Her muscles ached; she was always shivery. Now she worried about delivery!

Doctor must have dearly despaired over the patient he'd repaired.

Tension mounted, the due date came; he's wanted to see the football game.

At last she tried to cooperate. 'Til after the game, she was able to wait.

The long-awaited day was fact; our drama entered its third act.

Remembering several of his patients' gripes

Of doctors and hospitals and other types,

Our doctor-hero saved the day by just being there with things to say.

Good news for all... the wait was brief. Baby Kay arrived – what a relief!

His patient delivered just like a peasant. The doctor thought it was almost pleasant!

Then our OB's smiling face was proof to everyone at that place,

That despite the hard work he had done, he could now say,

"The battle's won!"

The patient, though, was still a pest. (She's had too much time to rest!)

Doc thought that he'd be left alone, but once again she had to phone.

With hemorrhage here and other pains there,

And nerves all tangled everywhere...

He listened again, and thought, "Oh brother! It's either one end or the other!"

That brings us up to the present date...an evening out to celebrate.

We think we have a good excuse for going out and cutting loose!

The patient has a souvenir to remind her of that fateful year.

Her scar beats any photograph; but doctor, where's your autograph?

Now if, in busy years ahead, this episode from memory's fled,

Re-read this rhyme of times so drastic...

When Mary burst her epigastric!

Mary Roush,
February, 1963

I then returned to Sweet Adelines and participated in our annual show in February, 1963. I was gradually regaining strength and a little much-needed weight. The family resumed its normal pace. However, it was not long before Skip received a major promotion as Food and Beverage Manager for the well-known Philadelphia Marriott Hotel.

Again, he would commute by train, live at the hotel and look for a home where we would move to, once the school year ended three months later. Skip came home on weekends, then back to the train station to leave again. Meanwhile, the girls were enrolled in a Catholic school in Arlington, and they all met many other neighborhood children and joined in the snow/sled fun in the hilly area where we lived. The girls were involved with scout activities so they met many new friends as well. One weekend, we all visited Philadelphia and stayed at the hotel so we could look around the area and find a house not far from a Catholic school. We were so lucky to find a great tri-level house with an acre of land, in the small community of Gulph Mills. Our realtor assured us of the school bus which also picked up the little boy who lived next door. A funny memory that comes to mind is the day we actually drove away and, as we passed the Union Station, Michael began to cry because he thought that was Philadelphia since that's where we took daddy every Sunday!

We went to register at the Sacred Heart Parish School in nearby Bridgeport, but discovered something we had never heard about: National Parishes. There were four others in the same town. And we were at a Polish Parish - neither of us with even a drop of Polish blood in our veins! There were no Catholic Norwegians! We were devastated, having bought our house with that stipulation, but not knowing the boy next door was from a Polish family. Dear Father Sokol, recognizing our plight agreed to let the children enroll, but we would pay tuition. And so, Mike and his sisters learned many prayers in Polish!!

I had hoped to transfer to a Philadelphia area Sweet Adeline Chapter, but all three were miles from where we lived. However, in the autumn when leaves fell off the trees, I realized there were many other homes in the area, and I assumed there must be several men who sang Barbershop with their local Mainliner's SPEBSQA chapter. So, perhaps there were wives who were familiar with the craft and the idea of starting a new chapter kept twirling around in my head. Not knowing what a full-time job that would prove to be, I set about acquiring a membership list from the men's chapter, and wrote to all the wives to see if they might enjoy starting a women's Sweet Adeline Chapter. There was such a positive response, we all started meeting together to plan the adventure of inaugurating "The Valley Forge Chapter of Sweet Adelines, Inc," which we chartered on Washington's Birthday, 1964. Our search for a qualified director resulted in finding Jim O'Toole, who had extensive experience in Michigan prior to moving to Pennsylvania.

All this time, however, I continued to take my prescribed medications and had begun daily drinking, which I see now, released so many inhibitions. I would take on any challenge and fulfill it to perfection. With meager dues from our 24 Charter members, I had purchased a copier which we called "Dora, the Ditto Machine," and it was ensconced on our table in the dining room where I could print out reams of information for the members, plus a weekly newsletter! The more I experienced the effects from the pills and drinks, the more I had to present myself as the capable, energetic, suburban housewife, as described in all those women's magazines. Those were the days before permanent press, and my five girls and one son always presented a perfect appearance. When they came home from school each day, I had fresh baked cookies or cake, further proof of my capabilities.

FEELINGS: frantic, inadequate, fear, shame, guilt, unworthy, bad...

Although the old piano still remained in the basement, we did occasionally gather around and sing the old tunes, despite the poor tuning by now, and impossibility of repair. I was still music-starved, and began to look at home organs. At one time, we had both a Wurlitzer and a Hammond organ in our living room so I could compare and decide which one I preferred. The Wurlitzer won out and it proved to be the perfect outlet for my inner turmoil of Feelings I didn't even recognize. I just knew I was a bad person and my anger would erupt continually in response to anything my husband said or did, to match his own growing anger and frustration. Late at night I could turn off the amplifier, put on ear phones, and play to my heart's content as I sipped from the fortifier in the glass on the top of the organ. Everyone else stayed asleep, hearing nothing.

I was still so excited about the recent purchase of our beautiful Ethan Allen console stereo. I could be surrounded by music, and store those records in the also new Ethan Allen record cabinet! I would play music from any style - classical to rock and roll - and entertain the kids at dinner, singing along and strumming a tennis racket (!) to the tunes of "The Monkees!"

Drinking became a daily habit and I worried that I couldn't make myself stop that urge. I knew nothing about alcoholism other than what I had seen in a movie, "Lost Weekend" or "I'll Quit Tomorrow." How could I relate to a prostitute who drank in bars, or a man who hid bottles in a chandelier? So I developed a new routine, and would get groceries at the A&P and then stop at the library around the corner to check out books on alcoholism. From there, I stopped at the State Liquor Store up the street, to buy more of that the magic liquid that helped me get through all those lonely days, with my husband retreating to work 12 hours each day, and the children arriving home from school at 4:00 pm. I devoted maximum energy to my Sweet Adeline duties and spent hours on the phone, always with a drink and a cigarette to accompany the calls as I sat at the corner of our kitchen table. I would devour those books to make sure I wasn't an alcoholic, but one word hit me hard: "Telephonitis!" Whoops...so I stopped reading and waited until noon to pour that first drink. Alcoholics even drank in the mornings! The only time I ever saw a "drunk" was when my Senior Class took their annual trip to Washington, DC and then to New York where the nuns wanted to show us off to another Dominican Academy there. The bus driver pointed out various points of interest, and made a point to tell us those ragged men in the doorways and alleys were alcoholics. That image made a firm impression in my memory, so how could I relate to that?

One thing that happened was that, because my inhibitions were so drugged, I became enraged at the Catholic school, when the kids told me about taking those old and familiar to me, Diocesan Tests. The nuns were walking the aisles, pointing out errors as the children wrote answers to the many questions. I was already angry enough at the Church after my experience at Georgetown Hospital and their near-impossible task of birth control, and my deepest fears about any possible new pregnancy. At this point, however, I called the Philadelphia Cardinal's office and complained bitterly and thereby removed the children from that environment and registered them in the very highly regarded Upper Merion School District schools. Karen was already attending Villa Maria, a Catholic Girls' Academy, much like my own history, so she wasn't affected by all the changes.

Life between 1964 and 1967 is all a blur, a "grey-out" with sporadic memories. High among them were the sounds of the children laughing and playing with our neighbors in the wonderful, large outdoor pool next door that Mr. and Mrs. Berry had erected for everyone. The Kenney family, with their six children, moved in right around the corner about the same time we did, surrounding the childless Berry's with 12 new young neighbors. They were so delighted with them all; I think they saw themselves as foster grandparents of a sort. I usually didn't participate in those backyard get-togethers, but would remain at home, listening to the fun, but feeling too depressed and ashamed, loving my children and determinedly keeping up their "good image," despite my being such a bad mother.

> "When we are all wrapped up in ourselves, we present a very small package to others."
> –Georgette Vickstrom

Somehow, in all my methods of escape, I read something by Edna St. Vincent Millay, and her words struck my very soul. I found two little paperback books of all her writing, and voraciously read and re-read every word. I even typed 25 pages of some of my favorites, so I had those verses readily available and with me wherever I might go. Two of them spoke of my truth:

> "My candle burns at both ends, it shall not last the night,
>
> But ah, my foes, and oh, my friends, It sheds a lovely light".

The second:

> "Come and see my shining palace built upon the sand...
>
> Safe upon the ugly rocks the solid houses stand..."

Such a Romantic. Much later, my sponsor and life-saver friend, Jack Roak, laughed when I told him about it and he added, "Of course, she was an alcoholic!" More recently, I read her total biography and identified with her story in such a sad, hopeless way.

As I was saying, I became totally unaware of how "not present" I had become to my family, depending on the girls to take care of themselves, especially young Kay. Kathy later told me she was so afraid that when Kay began to talk, she might call Kathy, "Mommy."

Skip and I were constantly fighting, and he stayed at work longer and longer. By then, he had become the General Manager of that greatly expanded Marriott Hotel. This was a real honor because no other Food and Beverage Manager had ever achieved that kind of promotion. Those were the days of "payola," and because he purchased so much liquor for the hotel, without his knowledge, the salesmen would deliver case upon case of vodka or gin to our home! The garage was well-stocked! Another time at the A&P, I innocently bought some chances for a basket of "Cheer." I won! But the Cheer was not laundry soap. It was a whole supply of bottles of any kind of alcohol you could use to cheer you up!

In the meantime, I sought desperately for help. The priest offered prayers, the doctor gave me new pills, and we saw a counselor for several months to determine why I wanted to drink, and how Skip and I needed to communicate, knowing it was his fault that I had become so desperate to need chemical relief! I put all the blame on him, and unfortunately, taught that to the kids, something I didn't fully realize until many years later.

FEELINGS: despair, hopeless, suicidal, guilt, shame, remorse, abandoned...

One afternoon in March, Skip called to have me come and meet him and Mr. Bill Marriott, Jr. and his wife, Donna for dinner. They were coming up from Washington, DC to see the hotel. I had always been so impressed with Donna, the epitome of a delicate, beautiful,

Mormon mother. She was exquisite in her appearance at all times, with her lovely naturally blonde hair framing her delicate facial features. This was a "call to action" for me, and of course, I needed to fortify myself with a martini as I dressed in my finest, and then drove the Schuylkill Expressway (locally known as the "sure kill crawlway") down to the hotel. I think we had a lovely dinner, but the next morning I had absolutely no memory of any of it - a blackout - and I was totally mortified. What had I said? What had I done? That was the turning point. I was sick and tired of being sick and tired! I never did learn anything about that evening, and I'm glad for that.

It was March 31st, 1967, and I called Dr. Laughlin (another medical pill-pusher as I later discovered) and made an appointment for that morning. I told him - again - I needed help, not more pills. He told me he had just heard of a newly opened out-patient clinic in Norristown, an adjacent suburb. I raced home and called the number he gave me, and made an appointment for 7:00 pm that evening. I struggled through the day without a drink and showed up to meet an Intake Counselor. He was very kind and gentle as he asked, "And who are you?" When I gave my name, he repeated his question, so I said I was Mrs. R.D. Roush, then mother of six children, daughter of... sister of, etc., and even the Bass in a Sweet Adeline Quartet! Living by the principle to always "get it right," I was becoming frustrated at not giving the correct answer to his repeated question. And way inside, I knew I needed a drink! He finally relieved me by saying, "No...you are yourself...and that's OK!" Well, of course I knew that simple answer and tried to save face by telling him I knew that all along but had misunderstood his question, answering with a litany of roles I played. As I drove home I was re-playing that introduction experience in my mind. I found myself asking, "Who is Myself?" Then, in my mind's eye, I saw six year-old Mary Helen clutching her Shirley Temple doll standing on the porch of her grandparent's house, with a sad, quizzical expression on her face. It was then that I first realized I had lost "myself" years before and I told her I would work to find her again, because one person in the world had told me, "You are Yourself, and that's OK!" HOPE!

The counselor pointed back to a table in the large room, where a group of men were sitting, smoking (!), and laughing. He told me they were alcoholics, having an AA meeting. I had read a little bit about AA in my library books, and must admit that one horrible Saturday night, I sat on the floor with the phone directory, and called the local AA club, and the man who answered told me about two meetings in my area. I went to one and explained how much of a problem my husband had been, gone all the time, etc., and one of the few women at that meeting looked over and said, "My dear, perhaps it's you who are the problem!" I guess they don't understand, I thought as I left the group. I also planned to attend the other meeting which was held in nearby Bryn Mawr Hospital in a meeting room on the 2nd floor at 8:00 pm, Monday nights. I found my way, being sure to get there early to locate the right place. Before I entered the room, I saw many people in the room, and they were well-dressed, drinking coffee and talking and laughing. I told myself this couldn't be it. They don't look how I feel. I left to go home.

Experiencing the same type of banter and laughter at the table the counselor had pointed out, I was doubtful but curious. I agreed to make subsequent appointments with other therapists and psychologists who were on their staff, to try to not drink (!), and to enter a process of evaluation over the next few weeks. During that period, I met frequently with Jack Roak, a recovering alcoholic who hadn't had a drink in four years! I couldn't even comprehend that. I was totally honest with everyone I met, and agreed to stop taking the pills. Fortunately, I did that without any withdrawal symptoms, and as I reviewed all the pharmacy receipts for the past five years, I was astounded at the amount of money I had spent to "ease my stress!" Jack urged me to try to go a week without a drink and I eventually did that, except for Friday nights when I met Skip for dinner at the hotel, and one martini made it so much easier for us to communicate. How heartily Jack laughed at that, and he continually encouraged me to believe I could do it. However, on July 27th, it was time for the results of the weeks of counseling, and Skip was to come with me for the meeting with Dr. Cleaver, the psychiatrist who, with her husband psychiatrist, Dr. Unangst, had established the Institute I'd been attending. Sitting across from her desk, I heard her announce to Skip, "We think your wife has crossed that thin line into Alcoholism." I was furious and felt betrayed. I remember thinking, "I'll show them...I won't drink at all...and prove that I'm not an alcoholic!" Dr. Cleaver then offered me the opportunity to join a therapy group conducted by her husband every Wednesday evening. So, my original sobriety date was July 27, 1967. In August, our entire family spent a week at a lake in Eagle's Mere, Pennsylvania where we rented a house and we could have fun together. I was missing my therapy meeting and feeling inner discomfort, so I quietly took myself to a nearby chapel and just sat in silence for an hour.

In the meantime, I faithfully attended those Wednesday meetings - ten men and two women - all of us alcohol-free, and with Dr. Unangst as our facilitator. I felt very honored just to be in his presence, as he was so well known in the eastern medical community for his many publications, plus his and his wife's research and application of LSD for chronic alcoholic patients at their one-year-long in-patient treatment facility at the Norristown State Hospital. I learned all about the disease and admitted I was alcoholic, but not the kind that went to those AA meetings! By December, three of those men were dead: a suicide, a fall, and one with a mixture of a certain anti-depressant (Parnate?), alcohol, and blue cheese!

At Christmas, we hosted the annual Management holiday party at our house with great fun, also with sing-alongs with my Wurlitzer!

Skip had brought all of the liquor home from the hotel and I wasn't even tempted to have any. I really enjoyed myself, plus I could remember it all the next day! We were already making plans to attend the annual Marriott Management Meeting during the first week of January in Chicago. This was to be my first exposure to the "higher-ups" now that I was the wife of a General Manager. More exciting was the prospect of the first night's party to be held at The Playboy Club. The more I thought about it, the more uncomfortable I became, since I would be the only one ordering ginger ale. How embarrassing! So, when it came time to order, I decided just one martini would be OK, and I'd feel more like a part of the group. That became my pattern at every night's social function with no reaction. However, at the last banquet on Friday night, I ordered a second martini, and began to feel the "buzz," so I immediately stopped and didn't even drink the wine served at each table. Flying back to Philadelphia the next day, I wanted to order a drink, but all Skip said was "Do you think you ought to?" So I contented myself with tomato juice, and that was it.

The following Thursday was one of those typical grey, misty days that were the norm for Philadelphia's winters, and I was feeling depressed, dreading the call to Karen's Villa Maria Academy Mother Superior to tell her Karen would have to be absent the following week due to a much-needed surgery for the ovarian cyst that had been detected. About 1:00 pm, I remembered how safe those single drinks had been the previous week and Skip had neglected to get all the liquor bottles back to the hotel after the party. He was gone to Washington for some meetings, and I decided just one drink wouldn't hurt, and would help fortify me for the calls I needed to make. That one drink lasted until 4:00 pm when the children came up the steps to the kitchen and I saw myself just as I had been a year earlier - a drink, a cigarette, and the phone, sitting at the kitchen table and I didn't remember a thing from those three hours. I later learned I sold more ads for our Sweet Adeline show than anyone else, and got a prize for it! However, I was in shock and now I realized how I had lit that fuse 10 days earlier until it burned out with that first drink again. I remember calling the clinic and talking to one of the psychologists and said, "I just bought the First Step of Alcoholics Anonymous" and I realized I no longer admitted my alcoholism, but now accepted it, from my head to my heart. Step One: "We admitted we were powerless over alcohol and that our lives had become unmanageable." And that proved to be my last drink: January 11, 1968. Thus began my new life in Alcoholics Anonymous.

> "It only takes one person to change your life......You" –Ruth Casey

Just a few months later, I wrote this poem as I reflected on the last 12 months of my life:

Reflections One Year After My Call for Help

As the 30th of March draws near, I can't help but recall the same date – only just last year when my world seemed very small.

I cared so little for anything – least of all, for me...guilty, afraid, resenting the life I couldn't see.

"Name? Address? History?"...numbly, my answers came. (Who could solve my mystery? Who'd understand my game?)

My earlier tries for help had failed; I'd searched most everywhere; my heart with fear, despair assailed still cried, "Please, <u>someone</u> care!"

I waited in a straight-backed chair for whom? – I didn't know. Who were all those people there? My aloneness seemed to grow.

And then a man was introduced to conduct my "interview." No doubt already he'd deduced my reply to "Who are you?"

He took his place across from me – scanned my clean new folder; he settled back so comfortably; my hands grew damp and colder.

I answered his queries; sometimes, he'd write – then look at me and talk for a while. Was it his gentleness, his voice, that eased my fright? Or that "trust in me" look when he'd smile?

I sensed he understood my fear and knew each troubled thought. He accepted <u>me</u> and made it clear <u>I</u> might exchange what I'd bought!

And he very gently let me know he'd lost years, his home, and family!

Startled, I asked, "Can anyone show me how <u>I</u> could learn your ... serenity?"

Mary Roush,
March, 1968

As I described earlier in this book, I stared at those slogans on the wall, and stayed for my first meeting. There was one other woman there who gave me what they called, "The Big Book of Alcoholics Anonymous." First, she turned the paper cover inside out so no-one could see I might be "one of them!" And of course, that added to my already simmering shame. She was moving to Florida, so I never saw her, - or many other women, again. That was the beginning of a life full of AA meetings, leaving the children at home. I had taken each one aside separately and explained what I could about my stopping drinking and needing to go to meetings so those people could help me get well. I was told I needed a "sponsor" and of course, went right back to Jack Roak to take me under his wing and guide me into a life based on "The Twelve Steps," which would eventually lead me back to "myself." And so I became addicted to AA for a long time, working hard to learn all these new ways of doing life. Because I had read enough about AA, I knew that if I joined, I could never, ever drink again! However, my new Program friends assured me they would teach me a new way of life so I wouldn't <u>have</u> to drink again. However, as I grew, my personality began to change and Skip reacted with anger, resenting that he could no longer know the Me that I was. He wanted no part of Al-Anon (a bunch of women), and our life became a full-time battle, in front of the kids, of course, as I was still playing that blame-game in the beginning months. Jack worked with each of us, getting to know our whole situation, and he kept telling me, "Buy yourself some time... buy yourself some comfort!" I was never really sure what that meant, but I was working to live by those simple slogans, taking first things first, letting go and letting God (?), keeping it simple, etc... My brain was so toxic, it was a year before I could read a page in the Big Book and retain its meaning. At every meeting, I took notes, an effort to study and learn. Once, we met with Dr. Unangst and his wife at a room at the hotel as they tried to help us adjust to this whole new experience. Subsequently, they converted the second floor of a barn on their country property and began conducting "Souse and Spouse" therapy groups every Monday night and Skip agreed to attend. He figured he would have a place and people as an outlet for his frustration. So he would come home early from work and I would join him in the car and we rode in silence out to the barn where we each went to our separate group rooms. Afterwards, we would stop at Howard Johnson's for a hamburger and we could talk about other people and couples in our groups, but never about ourselves. After several weeks of this routine, we were enjoying our sandwiches and he looked up and said, "You have to understand how hard this has been for me to be married to three different women: the one you were, the one you became, and the one you're becoming." That was an amazing conversation and I could see a little bit of what he was meaning. That was the beginning of a somewhat better relationship. We agreed to follow Jack's advice about how to communicate with a silly little ritual we practiced every Sunday at 2:00 pm for an hour, totally by ourselves with no phones or TV to interrupt. It was not until many years later that I realized the full impact of his words.

> "I shut my eyes in order to see."
> –Paul Gauguin

Jack assured us that he thought our marriage was worth saving, but one Friday, something had really gotten me into despair, and I sat on the porch of Jack and Dottie's house (Dottie had 10 years of sobriety(!), and was the Editor of the Main Line newspaper), waiting for Jack to get home so I could unleash my frustration and tell him I wanted a divorce, even though I knew that having custody of the children as an alcoholic mother would take the skills of a very good attorney! I was afraid I would go back to drinking if this life continued (more blame). He listened patiently and then asked me to think it all over during the weekend, and if I still felt the same way on Monday, he would help me find a good Philadelphia lawyer. In AA, there was a well-known admonishment not to make any major moves, jobs or decisions for the first 18 months. And I had only 10 months at that time. I have no idea what happened that weekend, but when I had 18 months, I looked back and realized God had done for me what I could not do for myself, and the rest is history.

> "All you need to do in order to receive guidance is to ask for it and listen."
> –Sanaya Roman

Earlier in my first year, I attended a weekend silent Retreat at a Catholic Retreat Center in town. It was for women from AA or Al-Anon, led by a recovering alcoholic Catholic priest and I remember asking, "What is willingness?" I was so confused at that time. I remember sitting on the ground beneath a tree, writing in my notebook, trying to prove that I was lovable, that God had created me through His love. I began to think about a "Higher Power" and considered the AA groups as that Power who had loved me back to life. I was remembering in my 1st grade Catechism book the first question was, "Who is God?" and the simple answer, "God is Love." Hmm... The paper I wrote was almost a mathematical equation, using as a metaphor, all the love I experienced making that beautiful brocade dress when I was in Detroit. Therefore, if God created me out of His love, then I must contain it within me. I had never really known what the word meant and never heard it used in my home. Here is that journal entry:

Thoughts and observations written after a Saturday morning Retreat Conference in Philadelphia, July 27, 1968:

What and <u>who</u> is God as I understand Him? ... what is my relationship to God? ... How do I think of Him and relate to Him? ... God is <u>not</u> a source of fear, nor is He an omniscient magician ... our concept of God too often remains as it was taught to us 25 years ago ... have I continued to think of Him as fearsome and aloof? ... God creates out of <u>Love</u> and each of us is a product of His love ... therefore ...

If I am to "create" something with which I am satisfied and happy, it will be an object of my love, and I will continue to have a special love for it, and take special care and pride in its future use. What more valuable a goal then, than "creating," as it were, my <u>new self</u>? True – I was created by God; I am an object of His love. He found pleasure and beauty in me, His creation. He cared for my "future use" – but, unlike an ordinary created object, He endowed me with a conscience and free will. He could not control my every movement and continued growth. I, instead, reacted and grew more as a product of my environment and willful desires, fears, emotions, and needs for physical survival. God did not leave me or ignore me as His loved creation. He has always watched and waited – and, as I can understand now a bit better, - He has allowed me to wander so far away that my own basic instinct for survival has this time turned me back toward His direction. It was not my intent to find God when I stopped drinking. That was merely the beginning of discovery. Slowly, I'm starting to grasp and <u>believe</u> things I've always <u>known</u> but ignored. Now I recognize the true answer to the question, "Who am I?" is the simple *word, "Myself" as I've learned the past year. But now I see better that "myself" was first made by God's love – then it was distorted and misused until it was hardly recognizable as God's product.*

...just as with sewing – making a lovely dress of beautiful rich velvet – the dress, completed, to last "forever" ... yet it somehow soon proved not to fit here and there. Letting out a seam – moving a button – perhaps even adding a jacket – changing the appearance altogether --- all these adjustments helped to cover and conceal --- but underneath it all, the original, made-to-last creation ... the dress of beautiful rich velvet ... "myself."

Seeing this better now, I can perhaps start to "re-create" myself – with God's help and guidance. If I am the <u>product</u> of His love, I also then, am <u>possessed</u> of love. I do <u>have</u> love as a part of <u>me</u> – woven as part of me just as the special "something" which gives velvet its rich lustre and beauty. Therefore, that sustaining love can be <u>used</u> and enhanced in my quest for my <u>original</u> "self." Though I find it difficult to know how to use those threads now, since I see them so dimly, if <u>I</u> try, and ask God to help guide me along – I can slowly remove all those extra seams, buttons, - even the jacket and cloak which have in truth been a camouflage, not an enhancement. It's going to be difficult; already I've discovered how comfortable these shrouds had become. How safe and secure they've seemed. If I can continue to <u>try</u> to learn to have <u>faith</u> in God's love – to <u>let</u> Him help me – I feel He will also let me know, in many subtle ways perhaps, that He is continuing, as always, to work His will for me through that love which was His to give from the very beginning of "myself."

(God, please help me let You be Yourself in me so that I can be myself.)

Mary Roush,
July, 1968

Once, when we were leaving mass, I spotted a rack of pamphlets and quickly pulled out two quarters to buy John Powell's *"Why Am I Afraid to Love?"* and began to study the definitions I could find. The best for me was written by Erich Fromm in his book, *"What is Love?"*

His definition, which I've never forgotten, is that "Love is the active concern for the life and the growth of the one who is loved." And that is certainly what defines the 12 Step Program of Alcoholics Anonymous, and many other 12 Step groups who loved me back to life!

After coming home from a meeting one night on Oct. 2nd, 1968, I was met at the door by Kathy, who told me to get right over to Montgomery Hospital in Norristown because Karen had been in a bad car accident. Skip was already there, and I watched as the nurses were cutting off her dress - one of mine she had borrowed that morning. Her best friend, Lori, was driving the car when they were hit head-on by another car on a rain-slicked road. This was a year before seatbelts, and because Lori was only 5'2", the front seat was pulled forward, which meant 5'10" Karen was sitting sideways in the passenger seat. Her head had hit and broken the windshield, and her right knee had smashed into and bent the dashboard, causing severe damage to her hip, with the head of the femur fractured with pieces of bone embedded in the acetabulum. After surgery, she was confined to the hospital but was finally released, with crutches, as she returned to her classes. This was the beginning of many surgeries she would endure for the next 35 years. She had already had to have an ovary removed the year before due to a benign tumor.

One time during my first year, I had sunk into a debilitating depression and wanted to just lie in bed. Then I received a phone call from a dear AA friend, June, who was severely disabled and lived in Norristown. She was going to be unable to attend that Friday night's meeting, but was asking me to please give a special message to Sam (one of the male gods of the AA clubhouse in Ardmore, my second home, it seemed!). So, of course, for June, I'd do anything and I forced myself to sit up in bed, and, pulling on my stockings, I remember muttering, "Please, God." As I drove away, I knew I really wanted to drink, even though I already knew that however bad I might be feeling when I went to a meeting, I always felt better when I left. This time I wanted to prove it and would get a pint of vodka to have in the car, just in case I still felt so awful when I left the meeting. There was time to get to the liquor store very near the clubhouse ("319"), and I had to get to the other side of the street and then parallel park (!) before I walked back, counting my money to be sure I had enough. As I approached the brightly lit State Store and went to open the door, the sign there said, "Closed...Good Friday!" And, I swear I saw standing on the other side of the door, a "Mr. Clean" image, arms folded across his chest, laughing and laughing! I "came to" then, and, grinning to myself, found the car and drove to the meeting! Hmm...I had said, "Please God," and discovered He had a great sense of humor, with the joke on me!

Eventually, we outgrew our house, and purchased a brand new, two-story, six bedroom house in Radnor, so I had new challenges to decorate, sew, and enjoy our deck in the trees around our hilly acreage, and met many very nice neighbors. The kids made lots of new friends at their schools, and we even joined a nearby swim club for more summer fun.

There was still some tension between Skip and me, and I really looked forward to joining my new AA family frequently. At one night's meeting, the topic was, "Do you take your meeting home with you?" As I drove into the garage later, I was aware that my whole inner assuredness and comfort was replaced by a dull ache and passive silence. That experience helped me immeasurably as I began to <u>Deal</u> with my Feelings as I was beginning to learn what they were and how I could put names on Feelings other than sad, angry, or happy. I realized how much of our problems were due to my own ego and stubbornness.

> "You need to claim the events of your life to make yourself yours. –Anne Wilson-Schaef

I was able to participate and enjoy many of the Marriott special events, now having "the Wife of the Manager" status. Another role! I made sure I looked good and was, at last, enjoying my sobriety. The hotel had been expanded several times with over 700 rooms, plus beautiful ballroom space, with entertainers in the various dining rooms and cocktail lounges. My Sweet Adeline Chorus used the hotel for many events and competitions, resulting in sequins all over the carpets! Singing had become my favorite pastime and I even had joined a quartet, singing Bass. None of the other three believed I was an alcoholic (nor did my mother). I had been President and also "Sweet Adeline of the Year" and hoped my girls would enjoy learning to sing in harmony as well. We were all laughingly trying to learn "*Christmas Chopsticks*" starting with "Twas the night before Christmas" and that became a family tradition when one of them would sing just that word, "Twas...." and hopefully three others might remember their parts...to no avail.

In about 1969, a record by Andy Williams included a song, "*Sing a Rainbow*," whose words struck me in my heart as I tried to rejoin the world again. "Red and yellow and pink and green, purple and orange and blue...you can sing a rainbow too...listen with your eyes and sing everything you can see...you can sing a rainbow, sing along with me..." Somehow, those words helped me struggle out of the morass of my addictions, and I began to make amends to others for my behavior and I tried to forgive myself.

> "The life which is not examined is not worth living." –Plato

In 1970, Kathy was able to participate in the Rotary Student Exchange Program, and she left for Brazil for her junior year of high school, with total immersion in the Portuguese language and customs in a small town in the inland part of the country. While she was away, we also hosted a Brazilian girl and had many occasions, through Skip's Rotary group, to become acquainted with students from several different countries. Kathy's experience that year laid the foundation for what was to be a lifetime of affiliation with the beautiful Brazilian people.

The family in Gulph Mills, PA (1964)

Family trip to Eagles Mere, PA (1967)

CHAPTER 3
1971-1991

FEELING, DEALING

In 1971, Skip's reputation with Marriott had been well-established, and, in addition to the hotel management, he often worked as a Regional Representative, inspecting other hotels in the Marriott system. In addition, he was assigned to open the under-construction, St. Louis Marriott, across from Lambert Field, the city's airport. His biggest challenge was to prevent the movement already underway to unionize the new hotel workers. He was successful in that effort, aided by several influential St. Louis businessmen. As a result, he became well-established in the local society. As was the Marriott custom, Grand Openings were always big celebrations and this was no exception. Besides a replica of Lindberg's "*Spirit of St. Louis*" airplane, the well-known comedians, Rowan and Martin, provided many laughs and enjoyment for the hundreds present, culminating with the ribbon-cutting and official opening of the high-rise hotel and its top-floor, "Windjammer Lounge," where guests could socialize and have a view of the activities at the airport across the street.

In the meantime, Kathy was to return from Brazil that summer and, instead of re-joining her school's senior class, she found herself helping us pack as we made the big move to St. Louis after all those years. She had become accustomed to entirely different family cultures in Brazil, and it was difficult to re-adjust, plus move to a strange city! This, too, was to be part of long-term consequences in her later life. Kris joined Skip and me, to investigate what would be our new surroundings in St. Louis, and there was no question that we wanted to be in the Parkway School District, just west of the city. We were able to find a large French Colonial house with a mansard roof, six bedrooms, and an acre lot set back from the corner of the street in the suburb of Town and Country. We moved, and did our best to adjust to a whole different community, totally a contrast to the hustle and bustle of the east coast area! People actually said hello or waved as they passed by and it wasn't long before I discovered that I was actually driving only 55 mph as it was zoned!

Karen had graduated from Villa Maria, and wanted so badly to go to West Chester State College near Philadelphia to major in Physical Education.

However, she was denied acceptance into the program due to her fragile hip condition and the physically demanding curriculum required. During her hospitalization, she learned a lot about the nursing profession, and decided to go that route instead. So she entered nursing training at Einstein Hospital in Center City, Philadelphia.

It was very difficult for me to leave my AA family after four years, and I sorely missed being able to talk with Jack, my sponsor. I went to several AA meetings in the area, but felt so strange, as I compared, rather than identified. So, I went to AA but was not in AA. Now, Kay was old enough to start school, and Mike went to junior high, and for the first time, I had no children in the house every day! I had begun to wonder what I would do when this time occurred. Originally, I thought I would go back to nursing, but now I was curious about this Alcoholism field, and began to inquire about local treatment centers and counseling, like my Jack! Then I saw a newspaper article about an eight week course in Beginning Alcoholism Counseling to be held at Washington University with the well-known, Dr. Laura Root. I couldn't wait to register and learned a great deal, and wrote many papers on different aspects of the disease, as she required. She called me to her office one day and encouraged me to pursue further studies, as my papers had indicated a real affinity for further involvement. Enjoying my new childless days, I decided maybe I could work at a job that wouldn't demand much, if any typing - a skill I never thought to learn at St. Mary's. Following a newspaper ad, I applied for and got a job as a receptionist for a regional oil company. I made it clear that if I received an urgent call from any of the schools, I would need to respond and the office was not very far from our home. So I learned to talk "adult talk" and would stay in touch with all the oil barges on the Mississippi, and adjoining rivers. It was fascinating, and I had so much fun talking to tug boat Captains and their crews, keeping up with the paperwork required, and working in a team atmosphere with others in the office.

Skip then received the word that we would move to Amsterdam and he would operate the Marriott Hotel there! We were all so excited and started to read and learn everything we could about life in the Netherlands. We were packed to go for our first visit and my mother had come to stay with the family, when Skip got the call that it was all cancelled! What a blow! It seemed that the corporate costs of moving our large family during a poor economic period was not a financially wise decision. I was totally devastated; I even tried to argue our case to the hotels' Vice President! Instead, they offered us the opportunity to take a vacation to any Marriott facility at no expense. So, instead of going to Europe, we chose to go to Mexico. We were at Acapulco, then Mexico City, and took advantage of tours and guides to help us learn more about their culture. Once, a driver we hired drove us through the mountains to the town of Taxco, with all its silver displayed in every storefront lining the hilly cobblestone streets. Then, we travelled further to Cuernavaca, a lovely village where we couldn't resist buying souvenirs. Back to Mexico City and its beautiful parks, and we even went to a bull fight! What an experience it all was, as we headed back to St. Louis with many happy memories, despite the circumstances that allowed it all to happen.

Some of the fun times for Skip and me were participating in other hotel openings around the country: New Orleans, Saddlebrook, NJ, Atlanta, Los Angeles, Santa Clara, Camelback, Portland, etc... The annual Management meetings were held in some exotic places with many fun activities for the wives while the men were in meetings. I enjoyed St. Louis and its people, but despised the weather with the heat, humidity, and the winter ice! However, some positives were the Arch, the St. Louis Cardinals, and some secret fantastic dining rooms in the warehouse district where you had to knock, and know the password before you could enter the lush surroundings where the fabulous steak dinners were among the best anywhere!

I will never forget the day Skip drove into the driveway in a Winnebago motor home, like the one we once rented in Philadelphia. At that time we had taken a two week trip, visiting each of the Great Lakes (!) with Skip driving miles and miles as we all enjoyed wonderful, memorable times, like when I was holding my dinner plate on my lap as I sat on the back bunk, raised my head and hit the upper bunk, with three-bean salad spilled all over me! We've laughed about that memory many times. It was unforgettable! Regardless, we had so much fun with the motor home, that when Skip saw one, hardly used and advertised, he pursued it and it became our extra home in the driveway, destined to become a favorite vacation getaway for our large family - even the dog - for the next few years.

One night, I received a phone call from my dear Jack, who apparently had been talking to Karen (!), and knew I hadn't really been active in AA, so he used a silly little "questionnaire" to remind me to get back to more meetings. That was to be our last conversation. I received word that the next day, he died of a massive heart attack. I was inconsolable, and made the trip back to Philadelphia for his funeral, along with at least 1,000 others like me, whose lives had been touched and saved by this amazing, humble man.

FEELINGS: grief, loss, abandonment, unsteady, mixed with gratitude...

After three years in the midwest, now we were to go further west, where Skip was being assigned as the opening General Manager of the brand new Denver Marriott hotel set to open in the fall of 1974. By now, Kathy had graduated and was enrolled in nursing school at the University of Missouri in Columbia.

But now, it was Kim who would have to miss her senior year at Parkway West High School, despite her outstanding work there. Even though our good friends, the Barlow's, invited her to stay with them for the year, I was very hesitant to have the family separated even more. By now, I had seven years of sobriety and as always, I guess, needed my family around me as much as possible. So, the decision was made and again, Skip and I flew to Denver to see the hotel which was under construction, and to work with a realtor to find a home in the Cherry Creek School District, which had been highly recommended by the faculty at Parkway. My first reaction to Denver was "Oh...where are the trees?" Such a shock then, but now they've become a hindrance to the ever-blue sky and the glorious feeling of space! As Skip was busy setting up his office, I went house-hunting and spotted in the distance, a green neighborhood and I asked to go and look there! We really were fortunate in finding a wonderful bi-level house with lots of space, an acre lot, an attached garage, and in the Cherry Creek School District. Once, while looking, the realtor asked who my husband would be working for. When I answered, "Marriott," he looked dumbfounded and asked, "What's Marriott?" So, Skip's work was to introduce this whole new brand of hotel to the west! What a challenge!

During the summer of 1974, we caravanned our way west with the motor home in the lead, and the sedan following behind, with each driver equipped with two-way radios so we could make/change plans across that flat, uninteresting land called Kansas. However, summers in that land can foster major storms and tornados, and we managed some frightening adventures trying to get two vehicles safely protected under bridges as the rain and hail pelted from above.

As we were unpacking in our new home in Greenwood Village, a southern suburb of Denver, I found myself sitting in my rocking chair with a city map and the AA Meeting Schedule, studying the nearest locations for my re-entry into active AA participation. Thank you, Jack! Little did I know then that I was being guided by other spiritual forces into a life I could have never before believed.

Unfortunately, soon after our move, it became necessary for Karen to leave her nursing school and come to join us in a hospital bed installed in our living room, and later a bedroom of her own for nearly a year. She had been "hipped" playing basketball at the school, and her very fragile hip made it impossible for her to remain for more on-your-feet training in nursing. After a year of rehabilitation and bed-rest, she chose to return to Philadelphia and start nursing school again...this time, successfully!

The hotel opened amid much fan-fare and Denver publicity, featuring a well-known skier skiing down the roof of the sloping drive-through entryway! The hotel was a quick success, and also became known for its cocktail lounge and the featured disc jockey, "Wolf Man Jack," drawing in crowds of people for music and fun.

Of course, I was meeting new and wonderful people in AA, and was asking around for any information about counseling training programs in the Denver area.

> "Life shrinks or expands in proportion to one's courage." –Anais Nin

I was directed to talk with a well-known woman therapist, Jo Wright, who was able to give me many suggestions and tips to pursue in my endeavors to learn more about the "ism" of Alcoholism - to be able to give back so much, as I had been given. That was how I learned about Metropolitan State College in downtown Denver, where they had a special School of Human Resources, with a specific course in Addiction Counseling. I enrolled and had to re-learn taking notes, and readying for exams, besides writing many papers. A whole different attitude about learning developed, along with an enthusiasm I'd never known before. It was in my Family Therapy class that we were required to write an autobiography. Having to put on paper so many pieces of my history, old, buried Feelings started to make themselves known for the first time, and at the time, I didn't have a real appreciation for the <u>Dealing</u> of those Feelings in order to really begin to <u>Heal</u>. That catharsis opened the door to what was to become the focus of my personal and professional life. I started to aim for a two-year Associate Degree, but once I got to that point, there was no way I would let myself stop this new, exciting learning process! I learned so much from teachers and books, but even more so, from my peers, many of whom were already working in the field of counseling. My required Internship experiences really took me out of my own comfort zone. For a long time, I worked on Skid Row with men off the streets and under bridges who needed to use our job bank, having to be sober first! They taught me so much about real addiction and all the losses they had incurred on their way to the Row. I also taught about and encouraged recovery to men with DUI charges, mandated to counseling and AA. There were very few, if any, women involved in alcohol-related offenses. Fortunately, I was paid nominal amounts by these agencies, and I was able to pay for my own tuition and books. That somehow gave me a very deep confidence and satisfaction as I was beginning to find "myself." Skip was very supportive of all my efforts, and interested in stories I told him about my experiences.

"Through learning to like myself, I've been more willing to understand others –JoAnn Reed

It was a happy time and Skip's association with the Colorado Hotel Association enabled our travelling to other resorts in the state, meeting so many interesting people, and learning many new things. He served as President of the Association and was also Chairman of the Colorado Convention and Visitor's Bureau. Another exciting event was our purchase of a lovely condo at the Keystone Resort, where we all had many great times enjoying the village and our lake views. The indoor hot tub gave us all wonderful opportunities to just relax and enjoy meaningful conversations with one another.

By then, I had nearly ten years of sobriety, and had become well-established in the AA community. I met dear women like Carole, Bonnie, Gini, and Diana who are friends to this day. In 1978, I was introduced to Betty Ford through a series of "coincidences" and, with three other women, visited the Fords soon after Betty moved back to their Vail summer home, having just completed her own addiction treatment. That was to be the beginning of over 30 years of visits, fun, sharing, and support.

The family had really begun to establish themselves in our new environment, and even I came to love the space, without towering trees to block my views of those blue skies and the distant horizon of the beautiful snow-topped Rocky Mountains.

The motor home provided many exciting trips around the state, camping out in lovely spots, and we came to dearly love Colorado! Kim had successfully graduated from Cherry Creek High School and was pursuing her studies of the Arts at Colorado State University in Fort Collins. Kris was enrolled nearby at the University of Northern Colorado in Greeley, studying Physical Education. We had all made a fun trip in the motor home to Philadelphia where Karen finally succeeded in completing her nurse's training, and she was working at a nearby hospital. Kathy continued her pursuit of a BS in nursing at the University of Missouri in Columbia. We used to kid each other by posting our grades on the refrigerator! And, in 1979, at the age of 48, I walked down the graduation aisle in my cap and gown and received my Bachelor of Science degree in Human Services. However, even more exciting for me, was spotting my brother, Bob in the stands with my family. He had actually come from New York for my graduation!

Skip made up his mind that he would no longer accept transfers out of Denver to other Marriott properties. Instead, the company decided to build a high-rise hotel in downtown Denver, and he would oversee the construction and eventual opening of what was to become a very successful hotel, drawing thousands for convention activities.

During all this time, I made my decision to go on to Graduate School for my Master's Degree through the School for Educational Change and Development at the University of Northern Colorado in Greeley. Since no-one was teaching anything about family issues in Addictions, I would be able to write my own course program and pursue whatever resources I could find and experience. At the same time, I was also deeply interested in the Employee Assistance field, after all my experience as a full-time intern in that arena for the telephone company. I gave them both great thought and consideration, but finally I had to commit my choice on my application for the school. When I reached that line, my hands seemed to take over somehow and I wrote, "Family and Marriage Dynamics in Addiction!" It was as if the choice was not mine to make. When my initial application was accepted, my challenge was to find the resources, measure the appropriate credit hours, describe the purpose and outcome of each pursuit, read specific books on Marriage and Family issues, and have written reports for them all. There was certainly no-one doing real Family Treatment in the Denver area. As one of my former internships, I was to conduct the weekly Family meeting on Wednesday nights for an hour (!) at a local treatment center. That consisted of meeting 40-50 women and children of men in the in-patient program there. I have to admit that the experience gave me even more incentive to actually pay attention to the dynamics involved and educate and treat families of alcoholics.

I had finally quit smoking when I had 12 years in the Program, December 31, 1979. That is how I unwittingly began to learn that "once the smoke cleared," I began experiencing sensations that now I had learned some names for...Feelings! I had contained them with cigarettes after I stopped drinking. The idea of using "medicators" other than alcohol to block all that pent-up Feelings energy that didn't fit into the normal "mad...sad...glad" categories, was a concept that didn't truly develop until the mid-eighties.

> "To experience a feeling is to open a window to our Soul" –Sarah Desmond

I was able to assemble a list of potential facilities to examine their Family Programs. At that time, Minnesota had become the hub of the treatment network, so the well-known Hazelden Treatment Center and their Family Program became the initial opportunity to start my training. During that program we were shown a video called, *"The Family Trap,"* presented by its author, Sharon Wegscheider. I was totally unprepared for the effect that 30 minutes of brand new information would have on me and my future endeavors!

I also experienced a Family Program at a hospital treatment center (where I'd once been a student!), but found myself now comparing two totally different approaches to treatment ideas.

On my return to Denver, I had opportunities to write reports on my experiences and conclusions at the time. Skip and my entire family gave me much support in my endeavors as I became even more aware of the effects of my own alcoholism and its effects on my own husband and children. Finally able to "Feel," I experienced deep remorse, guilt and shame, and I remember typing three to four pages in a letter to each of the children, trying to make amends for my behavior, specifically teaching them to blame their dad, just as I had.

Early in 1980, I went back to Minneapolis to attend the well-known Johnson Institute's three-week training program. I learned a great deal, and then experienced my very first immersion into group therapy with my whole class, facilitated by two therapists who were gently confrontive, as each of us divulged some of our own family stories. I was shocked and dismayed (Feelings!) to hear the word "caretaker" describing me! On the following break, I knew I needed something to quell those Feelings, and one of my motel-mates was in the process of lighting a cigarette, along with the rest of the class. I quickly went over and asked if I could have just one drag of her cigarette. But oh, it was menthol, a taste I'd never acquired even when drinking! So that was my one and only relapse from being smoke-free for nearly three months! And it wasn't until years later that I fully understood the dynamics of that whole experience; my hurt, frightened Feelings needed relief! Another new experience at the time, however, was that I was able to smell the ever-present lovely aroma of lilacs in the Minneapolis air...surprise!

I continued my research at other treatment centers; one was in California. Then, I spoke with a well-known EAP therapist, Pete

Parker, who had hired me as his representative at the local Coca Cola Company in Denver. He urged me to attend the Family Program at The Meadows, in Wickenberg, Arizona at no expense to me. I did so, as a member, not a therapist, and spent five very important days in my recovery. This was to be my first exposure to Experiential Therapy, and I was able to role-play in a scene where I knelt at the cot supporting a man who was representing my father. Little Mary Helen was able to finally release her pent up grief, anger, sadness, and betrayal to her dead daddy. Needless to say, that cathartic experience helped more widely open the lid that had contained so much emotion.

> "Let your tears come...Let them water your soul" –Eileen Mayhew

Having finally finished my research and papers, I completed and reported on the assigned books. But now, I had to face the facts and study and pass Statistics! That course was only available on campus in Greeley, at 8:00 am, Monday, Wednesday, and Friday, the entire summer. So, I made that drive back and forth, becoming a waving companion to the crop duster pilot along the way! I also was tutored by a senior high school student from Cherry Creek and lo and behold, I eventually took and passed the exam! After I passed my Orals, the day finally arrived when I received my Master's Degree in Science. As I received my mantle and diploma, I was thrilled to hear a loud "Way to go, Mom!" from the audience, which now included my mother, whom we had moved away from Columbus and into a retirement community in Denver, the city she always loved.

During my EAP internship, I met and got to know Dave and Jeanne Briick, a couple who formerly managed that same Meadows Treatment Center in Wickenberg, Arizona. They were brought to Denver by a wealthy philanthropist who received his own treatment with them. However, he then suddenly died from a heart attack, and the Briick's were searching for a place to start all over again. It seemed like a hopeless venture, and when I left for Minneapolis, we weren't sure they would still be there when I returned or perhaps they had gone back to Arizona. On my return, I was so pleased to learn that they had found just the place they wanted and had already accepted three new patients into Cottonwood Hill, in the northwest area of Denver. Even more surprising was the fact that they wanted me to write and facilitate their Family Program! I decided to attempt to meet that challenge and was finally able to put together what I thought were the best and most effective features of the programs I had attended. I mapped out a five day schedule, which was built around what I called, "List Work" in mid-week, where families and patients met for a structured communication event, learning how to identify and express Feelings, and listen, uninterrupted, to each other as they conveyed their deepest fears, anger, grief, guilt, remorse and hopes for the future. It was during this time that I attended a workshop in Colorado Springs, featuring the then well-known speaker/therapist, Sharon Wegscheider (whose "Family Trap" video had made such an impression on me at Hazelden). I literally hung onto all her words, and taped her talks so I could try to better absorb all these new concepts and dynamics of addictive families. After two or three additional workshops, taping, and note-taking, I met and talked with Sharon and she invited me to attend one of her company's (Onsite Consulting) "Family Reconstruction Workshops" near her office in Minneapolis. That was to be my first exposure to <u>real</u> Experiential Therapy with attendees physically ridding their bodies of stored-up emotional energy such as anger, grief, and guilt, much like my own brief but powerful role-playing with my father. After attending another Reconstruction, and Dealing with more of my own issues in the group therapy sessions, I could Feel I was Healing! Sharon invited me to work as an intern with a group leader in another similar workshop event, and I gingerly felt my way into a whole new and effective approach to therapy. That was to be the beginning of an over 20 year affiliation as a member of the Onsite Therapy Staff, working the five-day program in venues such as St. Paul, Palm Desert, Rapid City, Austin, Tucson, and Nashville. This was a blessing in the opportunity to meet and retain so many wonderful friends, fellow therapists who could all speak the same language and identify with as well as facilitate Healing for hundreds of others from all over the world. Most important, my friendship with Sharon grew deeper and more like sisters to this day.

Happily, my Family Program was becoming successful and well-known, and I admit the families taught me as much as I taught them! As part of the week with them, local Al-Anon groups would come to the hotel where we were housed and do a "meeting on wheels" as an attempt to insure the families' continued pursuit of Healing after this intensive week. After three or four years, I realized this was just not enough to better ensure families' deeper Healing, and began to consider going into private practice myself, and try to fill some of those needs. However, that was a frightening thought, considering everything that goes along with establishing an office, getting clients, covering insurance, and having the self-confidence to be effective. I met a very dynamic woman who became a sort of spiritual mentor as we met each week in her office. Sandy Myer-Brewer and I discussed at length my reservations as she encouraged me forward. One day, she totally took me off guard when she gave me her office key, and said she wanted me to take over some client work while she and her husband took a trip somewhere for the next 10 days or so! And, she had already scheduled my first appointment for the next week. On the spot, I had no choice, and said many prayers for the courage and ability to make such a leap into the unknown. That was December 23, 1983.

As Skip had always planned, when he reached the age of 55, he retired from Marriott and followed up on business interests of his own. Roush Management Company was born and he created his office in a nearby complex. Because of his outstanding reputation with Marriott, he was awarded a franchise to build his own Marriott Hotel and he chose Fort Collins, Colorado due to its potential market, and excellent location he found. So many of those restaurant napkins full of drawings and sketches were finally going to grow into blueprints for his long-dreamed-of hotel! Eventually, this beautiful hotel had its Grand Opening, and even Skip's high school friends from Lima, and of course, all our family and close friends were among the 300 who attended.

At our nearby new office, furniture was selected and office helpers hired. We all did a lot of brainstorming new ideas. It was an exciting era. Besides establishing an advertising agency as well, the next BIG step was the purchase of the historic *El Rancho* restaurant in the foothills of the Rocky Mountains just west of Denver. It was a large restaurant, and was a favorite of Denver locals who frequently brought their houseguests for an enjoyable dinner so they could see the magnificent views of the mountains. Now, with the hotel operating efficiently and successfully, Skip decided to convert the large upstairs of *El Rancho* into a lovely Bed and Breakfast addition. It was beautifully done, and became well-known in the community. Naturally, these endeavors took him away from the office and home constantly, with each facility in opposite directions from one another. After several unusual physical symptoms were noticed, a trip to our family doctor resulted in a diagnosis of Type 2 Diabetes and a stern warning to reduce the stress that all these activities were causing. But that was not possible at that time, as he continued to keep all his projects operating smoothly.

Having taken the plunge into private practice, lessening much of my anxiety, I chose to use the same space as my first office and learned to walk through my fear, with Sandy urging and supporting me. She also came and sat in on a few client sessions to give me feed-back afterward. Gradually, my self-confidence was boosted enough that I came to easily look forward to each day's appointment schedule and the challenges and opportunities each client brought into my cozy office. My calendar began to fill up through referrals, and one day when I hoped to go to lunch, I looked at my calendar and realized I had scheduled myself right through that hour! I quickly realized I had been trying to be a care-taker, not a care-giver. This was a major difference that could have led to burn-out unless I put myself into the equation! That was the beginning of my calendar readjustments that would assure me of lunchtimes and free Fridays! I had left my contract job with Cottonwood after four years, although they still called on me to train other family therapists. When they opened a new treatment program south of Albuquerque, they sent me there to train the new therapist to do my Family Program. One day, I heard from the Mother Superior of the convent at El Pomar, a conference center on the grounds of the Broadmoor Hotel in Colorado Springs. Somehow, she had gotten my name and knew of my practice, because she asked if I could consider conducting weekend workshops for Adult Children of Alcoholics and others who had grown up in dysfunctional family systems. This was exactly the target group I knew more and more about as I worked with Sharon's clients. I had also attended many workshops and conferences where I first heard Dr. Janet Woititz, from Rutgers introduce her theories of different adult traits that followed children from Alcoholic (or dysfunctional) homes, well into adulthood and relationships.

I really became intrigued by the idea, and contacted two friends/ therapists who were also part of the Onsite Family where we had been well-trained and aware of the very dynamics in question. We worked together to construct a therapeutic weekend, with attendees staying overnight at El Pomar Friday and Saturday. We began on Friday evening and closed Sunday mid-afternoon, having done much experiential therapy, culminating with a Saturday night fun festival! We commenced to advertise it, and suddenly realized we needed more therapists who, like us, had joined the Onsite Team over the years. The weekends were a huge success, with usually over 75 attending. We did one every quarter or so for two to three years. They were exciting, exhausting, Healing, and fulfilling! Our threesome-therapists, Lane Lasater, Verna Salmon, and I, then decided to expand our efforts and we became *The Colorado Recovery Group*, providing five day experiential healing workshops at a beautiful Jesuit Retreat House south of Denver. We limited the number to 30, with each of us having groups of 10 to work with through the week. I can remember so many wonderful stories about those days, being blessed to be able to facilitate hundreds of people from their inner secrets and pain into Feeling, Dealing and Healing! I must admit that all those people taught me more and more about myself, as my own Healing continued to progress. I was also very proud of the fact that I was earning my own money, and could buy appropriate clothing for my professional life. And I'm still wearing most of it! I was honored to be asked to do a video presentation describing "The Family System" as I had developed diagrams on a whiteboard to illustrate the roles of "The Family Trap," which I first learned from Sharon Wegscheider when I was at Hazelden. Dr. Nancy Downing, from Colorado State University, invited me to do the presentation, and I was able to get the basic points across in my 30 minute time limit. I guess that tape has floated around recovery communities since then, as I've heard, even recently, from others who have seen it and recognized me.

Besides all that was happening in my professional life, the family issues that were occurring became an exhaustive drain on my own energy at times. I think first of Karen, who called me one day to say she was worried about what was becoming her own proclivity toward drinking and she wanted help. Another highly regarded Onsite therapist was conducting an excellent program in Florida, treating others with addictions either of their own, or from their families of origin. I was so grateful I knew of such resources and Karen went there for Co-Dependency treatment. When it was time for their Family Program, I flew down to Florida and fortunately, was visiting and staying with other local therapists from our Onsite family. When it was time for Karen to talk with me about her experiences there and during her childhood, she divulged "the secret" she carried for 21 years. Years earlier, while I was hospitalized and quite ill prior to Kay's birth, the husband of the Irish housekeeper had taken the girls to their home for visits as he continued his business as a barber. However, he began sexually abusing Karen, warning her that if she told anyone about it, I would die! I was totally dumbstruck and devastated with that news and wanted to kill the man! My anger seemed to consume me, and I immediately placed a call to Gladys and Lacey's home in Virginia. I learned that he had died, and there was no reason to burden Gladys with any of this news at that time. It was a blessing that I was among other friends/therapists who helped me deal with my rage, wanting revenge, betrayal, and hopelessness, plus such deep sadness for my "little girl" who'd been abused in so many ways by all that happened. Soon after returning to Denver, I checked with Kathy and Kris to see if they also had any memories of such behavior. Kathy only recalled peeking through the keyhole of the locked bedroom, knowing something not good was happening. She also became a vicarious victim.

"Those who do not know how to weep with their whole heart don't know how to laugh either." –Golda Meir

Another fortuitous event was my being asked by the Cottonwood owners to go to Tucson, Arizona in 1985, where they had purchased a lovely desert ranch and were converting it into what was to become *Cottonwood de Tucson*. They again wanted me to establish the Family Program and train its staff. During my visit, they hosted me by visiting well-known tourist spots in the area, and on the way to see the art colony at Tubac, they commented on passing a small community, saying, "Oh yes, that's Green Valley!" And here we are!

It was during this time that Kathy and Alan's first child, our grandson, Brandon, was born, but only survived a few short hours. We later learned his death resulted from some kind of congenital heart defect. He was taken to Denver's Children's Hospital after Kathy and Alan's shocked traumatic hearing that their long-awaited little boy was not to be, after all. Grief-stricken, they wanted one more time to see their son and, together, mourn his loss. I drove to the hospital with four of Kathy's siblings, and we were given little Brandon, wrapped in a cold blanket as his body had been placed in a freezer, pending autopsy studies. I will never forget the feel of that cold blanket wrapped tightly around the body of my dead grandson. I specifically remember the kind nurse who lovingly handed him to me, assuring us that the warmth of the sun coming through the car windows would help take off that chill before we got to Kathy's bedside. Then, after his parents' loving and tearful good-byes, I took the baby back to the other hospital, but again, not alone, surrounded and supported by Brandon's would-be uncle and aunts. As shocked, saddened and grief-stricken as I was, I will be eternally grateful for my Feelings of love and support in the shared grief among all our family. Poor Grandpa Skip was in the middle of very complicated financial dealings in Fort Collins, trying to concentrate on his tasks while he grieved – alone.

Kathy's next pregnancy ended with the same horrific outcome as her brother's! Clare and Brandon both had funerals and were buried in a lovely spot in a Denver cemetery. After three other miscarriages, and Kathy's nearly suicidal depression, she and Alan were blessed by the arrival of Carrie, who is now a lovely 26 year-old graduate student.

The other sad event was the death of my mother at 89, when her body finally gave up so she could move on to be with her husband, and regain mental health after the prior eight years of increasing dementia and residence in a nursing home not far from our house.

As any reader might have ascertained, I have stopped separating out words to describe my Feelings, as they are no longer separate from me. By reaching this stage of Dealing and Healing, I can now live with and express myself as a normal part of my life!

"What doesn't kill me ...makes me strong."
–Albert Camus

Family Fun in Denver (1976)

"Way to go, Mom!" (1981)

CHAPTER 4
1991-2011

HEALING

My practice continued to grow successfully; however, I was becoming increasingly concerned about Skip's health, his weight gain, no exercise, and Diabetes. We decided to purchase a home in Estes Park as a weekend get-away and a good investment. "The Ridge," built into a mountain at 8,300 feet, had breath-taking mountain views and plenty of room for company. We both decided to not work Fridays anymore, and each weekend we made our 90 minute trek up to our new haven and we worked hard at fixing it up with new furniture and paint and in particular, building an enormous deck around a tree and a boulder, then stretching out to a point supported by beams buried into the mountain-side. The next year, we really splurged and had a large hot tub hoisted over the 75' long roof, and placed on a side deck adjoining one of the bedrooms. How fondly I remember sitting in that swirling hot water at night, hearing and smelling the wind in the pines. All the family and many friends came to spend refreshing time with us and often we tilted back the deck chairs, wrapped ourselves in all the afghans the girls had made, and watched for all the satellites in those clear star-studded nights. It was such a memorable time for all of us. Unfortunately, it was around that time that Skip's mother, Grandma Hoffman, passed away after spending her last two years in another nursing home not far from our house.

We made many wonderful friends in Estes Park, and my Newcomers' Club activities provided several social activities as we spent more and more time there, with Skip travelling back and forth from Estes Park to Denver, Fort Collins, and Evergreen. Once, we actually took a week away from work (!) and visited Sedona, Arizona...in January. Friends had been there and told us of the beauty and amazing colors and rock formations. Thinking Arizona was a warm/hot state, we were really surprised to find temperatures there even cooler than Denver at the time! However, the blue skies and daily sunshine - and sweaters - provided a beautiful week of exploring, touring, and becoming hooked on the area.

A big event for me was our hosting a family reunion of all of my Shay (my maiden name was originally spelled, "Skjeie!") relatives whom I had lost when we left Duluth. It was a big success held at Skip's hotel. About 40 family members arrived from California where most of them had moved to. Even one of my lost older third or fourth cousins from Norway made the journey!

In the summer of 1994, we planned a reunion of our own family, and Skip provided the air fares and housing for all of us at Sun Valley, Idaho over the July 4th weekend. That was great fun, and we all toured, hiked, golfed, and went boating on a gorgeous mountain lake. We were even able to watch many famous professional and amateur ice skaters practicing on the well-known Sun Valley Inn's ice rink.

Those reunions served as the highlights of what was to become a horrendous experience. We later learned that a management team member of Skip's had been "cooking the books" of the hotel and laying the groundwork - even spreading rumors among other members of Marriott Management - to force Skip out of the hotel. No matter how hard Skip's attorney worked on it, Gary had been so thorough, there was no way to find evidence to disprove these accusations, as the planning and setting it all up had been going on for over a year. After a long period of contentious, unsuccessful negotiations, Skip had to walk away from his long dreamed of hotel which had also absorbed our retirement funds, being targeted to grow and succeed with the Roush Management Company. My own reactions were Feelings of rage and betrayal (Feelings that years earlier would have generated a return to Scotch). But now, with new tools to <u>Deal</u> with life's challenges, I used my AA family and meetings to vent, journals to write, and prayers for support for both of us, refusing to let someone else take away my own inner Power! Our attorney cautioned me not to put out a contract on Gary!

1994 was full of stress and challenges, but as I've always believed, no matter how "bad" a situation seems at the time, an ultimate" "good" will result. Looking back now, I rejoice that my husband is still with me and he hasn't succumbed to the impossible stressful schedule he was trying to meet every day, draining more and more energy from his exhausted body.

Skip continued with successfully operating and improving *El Rancho* until one day a young couple - with deep pockets! - made an offer to buy the restaurant. After much negotiation, Skip was finally free to rid himself of the increasing stresses and we both decided to retire at the end of 1995.

To back up briefly, we did succeed in leaving our work duties after all the trauma, and we spent some time discovering southern Arizona. Originally, when Kim was in Scottsdale, we looked around that area for a possible winter retreat, but then she changed jobs and moved to New Hampshire! I remembered that Green Valley place that had been pointed out to me back in 1985, so we decided to rent a townhouse for a month and we "power toured" southern Arizona! All my earlier impressions of the state were dashed as we discovered the mountains and lush desert vegetation as we fell in love with the whole area. We agreed that when we sold the Denver house and moved to Estes Park full-time, we would arrange to avoid some of the mountain winter winds and snow, and spend three months in a Green Valley rental property from January to April.

So, after making the decision to retire, we went about the task of emptying out our 3,300 sq. ft. house of 21 years, putting it on the market, and having a huge yard sale, ridding ourselves of saved "stuff." We could take many items to the Ridge, and the children came to retrieve special items they wanted to keep. One of the things we finally sold and parted with was a very heavy lawn jockey statue we acquired in Philadelphia. It was the kind that used to stand at the edge of southern mansions' driveways. We had always treated him with great respect and placed him in prominent places in our homes. But there was just no place for him in the mountain home. Ultimately, we said good-bye to our offices and neighborhood, and moved to the Ridge that fall. We had already secured a three month rental in Green Valley for January, but learned each year when we returned in April, we were still subject to being snowed in and cut off from the one mile, one lane dirt road that wound itself a twisty, hairpin-curved mile from the main road.

We enjoyed a great family Christmas at the Ridge, but imagine our surprise when we tried to open a large, heavy, newspaper-wrapped package and, lo and behold, our little lawn jockey was back in the family amidst all our raucous laughter, thanks to Karen and the girls buying him from our earlier yard sale! He now resides with

Kim and Jeanne and provides many happy memories whenever we see him.

During those years (1996-2001?), we took advantage of Skip's cousin Mel's ambitious arrangements to plan tours to Europe for many of the Roush's in Lima, Ohio, plus friends (30 people). We visited the German origins of the Roush's, and toured so many well-known and wonderful towns in Luxembourg, Germany, Switzerland, and Austria. Mel knew a German tour operator who helped him plan the itineraries, guides, lodgings and many meals for a very reasonable price each time. We still play "remember when" stories about our wonderful memories and experiences.

In the meantime, we came to enjoy meeting and knowing so many new good friends in Estes Park, but came to love our winter respites in Arizona as well. During our three winter visits, we got to better know the area and advantages and disadvantages of different housing communities. Naturally, the many "Open House" signs gave us added opportunities to compare and consider, as we fell in love with the southwestern furnishings, colors, casual living, and glorious winter weather! But, one day in 1998, we walked into another "Open House" and immediately knew this place was something we each had been secretly looking for! This was a 1,800 sq. ft. house, above a golf course, totally private, and with phenomenal views of the Santa Rita Mountains just to our east. Our walled courtyard surrounded the house adjacent to desert wilderness around us, complete with flowering cactus and shrubs, and the sound of the many birds that came to love our bird feeders. The crumbs of leftovers on the ground let the Gambel Quail find food as they gave birth to their adorable little walnut-sized babies who would line up and chase after their mothers and other family members. Such a delight to watch, far different from the large families of elk who would cross streets in Estes Park much the same way! After much discussion and financial planning, we decided to purchase our first Arizona home. We would spend six months here and the other six in the mountains, becoming "Snowbirds" like so many others. The present owners did not want to vacate until the fall, when their new house in the nearby senior community, La Posada, would be completed. That was perfect for us so we could have our summer in Estes Park and then return for the closing and new keys in September. We were both truly trying to Heal from our years of disappointment and loss. This new adventure provided hope and focus, so we could look forward and plan decorating ideas and furniture. We found ourselves smiling more as the old heart heaviness gradually began to lessen.

> "True life is lived when tiny changes occur."
> –Leo Tolstoy

In September, Kay joined us for our trip to Green Valley for the closing, and we stayed at a motel while we surveyed our totally empty new house. I did major surveys of what and where to find furniture stores and had lists of names, addresses, and directions (!) as we explored Tucson where the first order of business was to get beds, linens, and some kitchenware so we could leave the motel as quickly as possible. Once that was done, we spent hours and hours looking at furniture stores and finally settling on our choices for the living room, den, kitchen, etc...All items had to be ordered and would not be available until December or January. So, we returned to Estes Park that fall and planned how to pack and organize for our first four months in the desert before returning for our next six months in the mountains!

Finally, we put everything together and moved into our Green Valley home and luxuriated in the mountain views, the layout, and finally the decision to rid ourselves of the glaring white walls. We painted each wall with different desert colors and blends. We had new draperies made for our living room walls of windows and added new lighting fixtures, etc... This was our only really "bare" new home since we first moved to Denver in 1974.

We planned to do the six/six month routine, and spent half years in the desert and then the mountains. It was the best of both worlds for three years. In the meantime, we made new friends in Arizona, and I found the local AA community to be most welcoming and rich with long-sober members having much to share with me as I continued to learn and Heal from past memories.

<u>KAREN</u>

Meanwhile, Karen was alone in her Denver apartment, still suffering from the severe chronic pain (RSD: Reflex Sympathetic Dystrophy) resulting from the medical error of a Cardiologist who performed an Angiogram through the right wrist site, yanking the needle out of her arm when it spasmed. This resulted in shredding the artery from the elbow through her right hand, causing immediate pain which was ignored by that doctor and subsequently explained by him as just "spasms." Ultimately, the pain was so severe and disabling, she was no longer able to work at her treasured commercial travel agent job as she was unable to use the computer keyboard.

Her intense pain led to many methods to try to create function in her arm, but to no avail. Her Neurologist prescribed all the necessary meds for pain and for sleep, with some tragic results. Having taken Ambien for sleep, she discovered that she was walking in her sleep during the night and would find her pill bottles opened on the kitchen counter in the morning. She had no memory of having taken anything, but remained groggy. If she went to the bathroom during the night, several times she would fall forward on her face, resulting in black and blue bruises covering her otherwise lovely face. By the way, many years later, Ambien was discovered to be very dangerous - and addictive - with others' stories of driving their cars, having accidents and strange events occurring with no memory of any of it.

It became apparent to us that she needed to be closer to family, so we purchased a townhouse not too far from us, and moved her out of Denver to be nearby. Unable to afford three homes, we were forced to sell The Ridge, with all its memories and friends in the mountains. We emptied it of all the furniture we could no longer use. Driving down the hill, away from our mountain retreat for the last time was almost too difficult to bear. To this day, whenever we visit Estes Park, I can't even allow myself to look up to see it nestled into Prospect Mountain.

And so, we became full time Arizona residents, and managed to learn how to deal with the summer heat and monsoon humidity. I joined the local Newcomers Club and became an active member of the AA community, now having over 20 years' sobriety.

Having been so involved and informed about the recovery and medical resources in Denver, I was at a total loss as to where to find help for Karen in the Tucson area. Fortunately, through a series of "God's Coincidences," I was put in touch with a Pain Specialist, Dr. Jennifer Schneider, and Karen and I were so relieved to meet her and follow her recommendations on treatment plans.

In the meantime, we heard of a doctor in Philadelphia who specialized in RSD, and Karen and I made another trip to specialists across the country for whatever help might be available. We had already several times travelled for medical help from California to Boston, searching for relief for her right hip fracture complications that had arisen from the automobile accident in Philadelphia when she was 16. In Philadelphia, I stayed at the high-rise Holiday Inn in a room overlooking the corner where our once enormous, beautiful Marriott Hotel of Skip's had now been replaced by an office building complex. More memories, more loss.

The stay at Hahnemann Hospital with the famous specialist resulted in no progress after two weeks, so we agreed to his advice to have a pain-deflecting device surgically implanted in the base of her skull, with a control generator placed under the skin of her upper abdomen. She then could use a hand-held device (like a computer mouse) to activate the generator to send electric current to the brain to interrupt the pain signals. That was helpful for a very short time after we returned to Arizona, but the device apparently shifted its position in the skull so it wasn't effective unless she held her head at a certain angle.

After our return and registration at the University of Arizona's Pain Center, we learned about a newer model of the embedded device. It would be a more solid fit higher in the skull. The very well-known and competent surgeon who specialized in this procedure was very confident of future success, so with great hopes and expectations, Karen underwent the surgery in September, 1998, only to return to her room with the device turned on to its maximum strength of electrical impulses going to her brain. None of the nurses knew anything about these implants and they were unable to help. Fortunately, I was able to find the "mouse" and knew how to operate it in order to turn off the current. The surgeon came to her room afterwards, only for us all to discover that she had no feeling on her right side. "Supposedly" there were adhesions around the previously installed device when it was removed, apparently causing trauma to the spinal cord. He assured us that the damage would heal within a year. In the meantime, she would have to spend time in a Rehab Hospital for extensive physical and occupational therapy. She spent the next six weeks hospitalized, learning how to use her hand and walk again.

Dr. Schneider then referred us to the best-known pain specialist in Tucson, Dr. Mitch Halter. At our first visit, he looked at her hospital charts as he entered the room and declared, "Oh, you're the one with the nicked spinal cord!" Those were new words for us and we all agonized over their meaning, and the denial by the surgeon of that type of injury. It was another medical error which ultimately led to her death in August, 2005.

The last seven years of her life were torturous for her as she tried to manage at home. No longer able to drive her car - or a golf cart, she was now having to use an electric wheel chair to get around her apartment. Unable to lie down, she lived in her recliner chair in front of the TV in her living room, or she worked at her computer where she made special stencils and business cards for others. Our very favorite card, which she made for herself said, "Karen Roush...Nice Person!"

As a result of all her sitting, she developed severe decubitus ulcers and was hospitalized again, this time in the Burn Unit at St. Mary's Hospital. She was plagued by these ulcers for many months and with much damage.

As I look back, those years were dark and frightening. It was a fight for survival for all of us. We had to give up the Colorado Rockies' Spring Training games each February with her cheering on her favorite players. Her love of baseball was unmatched and she had many collections of baseball memorabilia, knowing her Rockies team would "make it" someday! Coincidentally, it was during a newly organized Rockies game where she and her dear friend, Paul had shared season tickets, when she first felt some chest spasms which eventually resulted in her referral to the Cardiologist whose error was the beginning of the end. No heart involvement was found.

During the last 18 months of her life, Karen was in one hospital or institution after another since she could no longer care for herself, but needed ongoing medical attention. Skip and I made regular daily trips to Tucson to one hospital or another nursing home. It was a sad day when we realized we could no longer make payments on an unoccupied house. Karen participated in our decision to sell it and rid herself of "things." We carefully followed her directions regarding the disposal of her belongings. Kris and DD joined us in this painful endeavor. We took all of her jewelry to her to sort for what and for whom. The house went on the market, furnished, with the exception of her chair and the new large screen TV Paul had bought her the previous Christmas. Even her computer was totally erased for the new owners. Another chapter ended.

Karen's physical health continued to deteriorate from her neuromuscular illnesses. Her lungs were affected and every treatment brought on more complications of complications. During one of her stays in an ICU, she had to be intubated, unable to speak. She would write notes to us and her nursing attendants. Later, in going through her papers, I found some of those notes, even to: "Please turn off the fan." She was totally helpless and so difficult for us to watch. After all, parents are supposed to fix their children's problems! Both Skip and I became more and more depressed as we realized our helplessness. In near despair, I sought meditative answers walking a large labyrinth laid out on a ballroom floor in February, 2005, when I attended an AA Women's Conference in Las Vegas. Through some miraculous visions and messages, I heard what I needed to know: "Be there for her."...and I shared that experience with her when I returned to Tucson.

> "God must become an activity in our consciousness." –Joel Goldsmith

We all relied on the 11th Step of our Recovery Program: "Sought through prayer and meditation to improve our conscious contact with God as we understood Him, praying only for His will for us and the power to carry it out." In April, 2005, Karen celebrated her 18th Recovery anniversary. Each day as we ended our visit or phone conversation, our mantra was: "Every day...all the way!" Much later, to my surprise, I came upon a Gratitude List she kept throughout her challenges.

In June, for her 53rd birthday, her sister Kathy arranged to come for a visit and planned a session for Karen with "Glamour Shots," a service that was able to send a photographer and make-up artist, complete with costume accessories, to her nursing home bedroom! The two of them had great fun with the crew, taking nearly 50 pictures with poses from cowboy hats and scarves to beautiful poses, holding red roses up toward her neck and chin to cover her tracheotomy tube! When I took the proofs back to the store to order our favorites, the owner refused to take any money for this loving gift he'd "paid forward," after having received so much support and love from others when his sister died from breast cancer the year before!

Finally, in July, 2005, when I went to visit Karen in another ICU, she looked me in the eye and said, "Mom, I just don't want to play anymore," realizing that every new procedure being tried resulted in worsening situations. We all had to come to the realization of this inevitable outcome, and struggled with that final acceptance of God's will, and faith in His power to carry it out (the 11th Step again...).

We are ever so grateful for the loving support of Mitch Halter, Karen's doctor, who had overseen all her decline and would even drive across Tucson after office hours to visit her. It was he who declared one day, "No-one should die in a hospital!" and assured us that Hospice was the best answer, and answered my doubts that yes, they could provide the bed, the oxygen, pumps, etc. and she could spend her last days in our living room as she and her body began to let go. Karen's Spirit soared at the thought of being with us and all who loved her close by. She moved into her hospital bed at our home August 12th for her last 16 days, filled with the love and laughter of all our family and friends, and she was even entertained by quartets from my Sweet Adeline Chapter in Tucson who came down and sang to her in our living room. Even though we had had a distant relationship, my brother Bob from Columbus surprised us all with a visit one day. That was such a glorious gift, especially to me, deep-down needing my very own family connection, something I spent a lifetime searching for and creating in all our moves and re-establishing through so many moves.

We will be forever grateful for the help and support we received from all our friends, Sweet Adelines, and La Posada, as they brought food, hugs and love to all of us. My dear friend, Carole flew down from Denver to stay at her nearby winter home and she "took over" the kitchen and management of the myriads of needs that arose each day. Through the combination of Carole, our daughters, DD, and many Starbucks runs, we made it through each 24 hours. Thank you, God!

Kathy, Alan, and Carrie arrived from their Missionary duties in Brazil and Kathy, a Master's Level Nurse, was able to help the Hospice nurse tending to Karen's needs, meds, and treatments.

This was a very difficult, loving role she played with her older sister, which later became the roots of some severe depression and the ultimate end to their Brazil duties for a long time.

Looking back now, I see how all the loving prayer support from hundreds of people brought us the Grace to survive each 24 hours. Karen's best friend from high school, Lori, flew from Milwaukee to be with her a short time, and once the news of her situation reached all her Denver friends and Recovery Community, she began to receive emails of support and gratitude from so many whom she'd helped in their Co-Dependency recovery. She and I planned special gifts she wanted for other family members. She even left 12 thank-you notes in envelopes for Skip and me, each containing $50.00 for monthly dinner/movie nights for the following year! This was something we did on the 28th of each month, the anniversary date of her leaving. On that Sunday, August 28, 2005, at 2:55 pm, with Skip and me and Kathy and Alan with her, Karen gave her last breath and her Spirit was finally freed from that broken body and she could fly! I could "see" her leaving toward the mountains outside as I screamed, "You're free...you're free...you're free!" Then, removing all the pillows used to prop her body into some semblance of comfort, I threw them across the room, crying, "No more pain... no more treatments...you're free!" The next day, we were deluged with yellow butterflies all around the house. The cocoon was gone...

All of Karen's siblings and family were very special in our shared family love and loss as we prepared for her viewing, funeral, and cremation, as she'd wished. The Mass was said by our Pastor, Father Maldonado, who had formerly visited Karen in the hospital and at our home, declaring she had done more for him than he could ever have given her. He continues to be a dear friend for Skip and me.

There are so many memories I treasure of the 53 years I was privileged to be Karen's mother. Then, I remembered the first verse of that poem I saved among other favorite sayings, which we had been instructed to collect by Sister Francis Gabriel back at St. Mary's, "I'll give you for a little while a child of mine, He said... for you to love and care for, and mourn for when she'd dead."

> "I shut my eyes in order to see." –Paul Gauguin

Existing on shocked adrenaline, Skip and I took my long-planned trip to Rapid City for a reunion of sorts with former Onsite therapists. I don't remember much about seeing Mt. Rushmore or Sharon and Joe again, but when we returned to our empty home four days later, the reality of what had taken place in that living room hit hard, and we began the long painful grieving process: sorting things, collecting cards, emails, and funeral mementos to store in "Karen's Box." We spent Christmas with Mike and his family, and had a special baseball Christmas ornament to share each year with one of her siblings' trees in years to come. We acquired Karen's cremains, having reserved some of her ashes in lovely little memorial urns, mine, always on my dresser. The following summer, we went to Estes Park, and, following Karen's wishes, we spread her ashes on her special, favorite spot in Rocky Mountain National Park.

∽

After seven years of energy output, our bodies decided to express their toll by more medical complications for each of us in 2006.

My aching left shoulder became so painful, I required Rotator Cuff surgery in February. However, due to the total loss of the tendon during that operation, the surgeon had to do a "pec transfer" (pectoral muscle), which left me with limited range of motion in my left shoulder, but no more pain! I was singing in a Sweet Adeline quartet at the time, and for many weeks sang with my arm in a sling, no matter what kind of costume I was wearing, either to chorus rehearsals or quartet duties.

Also, Skip's ongoing severe back pain was worsening every day. Despite injections and therapy, there left no other option than to have major lower back surgery to fuse and implant a metal support device with six long screws to reconstruct the damaged sacral vertebrae.

After much deliberation and consulting with the highly regarded and recommended Neuro-surgeon in Tucson, the operation was scheduled for August, so any former plans to travel to Colorado were totally out of the question. The surgery was a great success, but after returning home, more severe pain and fever necessitated a 911 call with a trip back to the same hospital where it was discovered that he had a severe case of sepsis (blood poisoning), and was admitted to the ICU for several days. He was running temperatures as high as 105° and was very ill. Fortunately, Michael came to give us both much-needed support. By then, I was beginning to have real fears that I might have two sets of cremains to deal with. Again, all the love and prayer support we received from so many friends and family granted Skip the Grace to overcome the crisis and eventually, he come home to recuperate.

By that time, we were both totally exhausted and decided to take a very special two-for-one cruise in late November. TBT (The Big Trip) turned out to be a true God-send! After two nights in Honolulu, we flew to Auckland, New Zealand for a four day visit before we boarded our ship, Regent Cruise Line's, "The Mariner," for a 21-day cruise across the Pacific to Los Angeles!

That experience turned out to be one of the most memorable times of my life. As in most cruise ships, there are daily AA meetings held in a private room, listed on each day's activities schedule for others like me. Among the five others who formed that group, who should also be there but Paul Williams, the well-known lyricist and song-writer, who does not want to be "Anonymous," (with over 20 years in recovery.) He wanted to be available to many others in show business who might need his help. Our daily 5:00 pm meetings became very meaningful for all of us, including a couple from New Jersey, and two men from Vancouver who were partners. I was able to really share my feelings and pain about Karen's leaving, and the Friday night before we were to disembark in Los Angeles came to be a true blessing for both Skip and me. That was the night Paul was featured as the headliner for his own over-one-hour show in the ship's theater/lounge. After spending nearly an hour singing all of his well-known material with the full orchestra behind him, he announced that he wanted to dedicate his final number for a fellow woman passenger (!) as he looked at me in the front row. Then, his rendition of *"You and Me, Against the World"* was the tear-producing event, as he finished and looked up and said, "That's for you, Karen!"

> "Be still and listen to the stillness within."
> –Darlene Larson Jenko

The entire trip was a dream as we visited many of the Polynesian Islands and learned more about the native cultures and traditions, even being entertained at several festive functions along the way. We met several enjoyable fellow passengers, including Ernest Borgnine, another celebrity who entertained us on stage one evening with some riotous tales from his long life as an entertainer. We enjoyed frequent dinners with "The Mariner Six," and Paul's wife, Marianne.

After disembarking, we spent our first night ashore at a hotel near the airport and Mike and his family all came to see us. Then we enjoyed a great family dinner together at a favorite restaurant of theirs. Christmas came a few days later and our recent journey led us to agree that we both loved to "just cruise," if we had the means!

In the meantime, we were thoroughly enjoying our years in our wonderful house with its lovely patio and much-used hot tub! Our good friends from Denver, Carole and Bill Horton bought a winter home not far from us and became welcome seasonal visitors, so we've been able to share many fun winter activities with them. Other friends from earlier times found their way down for winter visits in our glorious sunshine; but the biggest event of all became our long-considered decision to rescue two adorable little dogs. They had been abandoned but each had found the other and decided to be a team, totally bonded to each other, but needing a loving home. So, Foxy and Fannie quickly became our "children" who continue to bring us so much joy and love! We have wondered what part Karen might have played in bringing them to us. Hmm...

Skip was invited to become a member of the Board of Trustees at La Posada, a well-known and prestigious continuing care center in Green Valley. We participated in many of their activities and came to realize that we might consider a future move. Board members are not permitted to live on the premises as long as they are active participants in the Board responsibilities. After much deliberation, we figured out a way we could afford to make the move, and, despite the very poor real estate market in 2009, we buried an upside-down St. Joseph statue in front of the house (!) and a "For Sale" sign found its place at our curb. We took a brutally honest look at our situation and realized we truly didn't need all of the 1,800 sq. ft. home we had come to love so much. We then were able to pick out a La Posada apartment half that size, needing a first floor location because of the dogs, and we were blessed to be able to sell the house with most of the furniture within ten days! That required a very careful discernment of how to down-size and rid ourselves of so much accumulated "stuff." As difficult as it was, we were finally "free" and went about furnishing our soon-to-be new surroundings. After seven years, Skip resigned from the Board, and we moved two weeks later, on May 15, 2009.

> "To accept the responsibility of being a child of God is to accept the best that life has to offer you" –Stella Terrill Mann

Unfortunately, I had already begun to experience several medical crises, starting with a fractured pelvis resulting from a fall to our driveway concrete as I attempted to pull a wheeled cart carrying trash out to the curbside container. Not allowing for the sloped drive, the cart attacked me (!) from the rear, throwing me forward to the street. Since it was only 7:00 am, no-one was up or around (Skip was away in Nashville). Realizing I couldn't stand and bear any weight, I'll never forget sitting down and scooting myself backward all the way back to my bedroom where I could reach a phone and call my dear friend, Sue, and then 911. She took all my adrenaline-charged instructions about phone calls and cancelled appointments, keeping my mind racing about all the complications. After the hospital diagnosis of a fractured left pelvis, I was warned there would be nothing to do but go through the pain of Healing and give time, time! After three days, I was transferred to La Hacienda, the La Posada Rehab Center for three to four weeks of therapy and learning to walk again. That was to be the first of many adventures that took me back and forth to La Hacienda! That was my "home" in the fall of 2007.

It was nine months (June, 2008) later that I tripped over a door jam and fell again, this time, the right side. Another 911 rescue, with a resulting diagnosis of a hip fracture, but only in the femur area, so the doctor could do a partial hip replacement placing a long strip of metal into the femur where the bone could come to adhere to the appliance. Again, a three week stay at La Hacienda for more time and therapy and re-learning to walk! As always, Kris and DD left Albuquerque and came to be of invaluable help!

It was not long, before I began to have extreme discomfort and pain in that right thigh. The surgeon ordered a major battery of tests, but apparently there was nothing to be seen as the cause. After what seemed like endless medical interventions, pain medications, X-rays, and even a spinal surgery to be sure there wasn't nerve damage, I was referred to one of the top Orthopedic surgeons in Tucson. After a series of would-be diagnostic X-rays spanning several months, Dr. Miller could finally see that the original "appliance" was loose and the bone tissue had never adhered to that metal. The result had been two years of unremitting pain, the use of a cane, and medications to help alleviate the discomfort, total frustration and depression. The solution was a total hip replacement.

However, I had also been diagnosed with Bladder Cancer which was requiring weekly chemo-like treatment sessions with Mitomycin, and then the stronger BCG in an effort to kill the cells. During the second six-week series of BCG, my body rebelled and said "NO!" and I was hospitalized with pneumonia, dehydration, and general malaise. Four days before the previously-scheduled hip surgery, I had to postpone, as I needed to regain enough strength to tolerate the surgery. Back to La Hacienda!

In the meantime, we moved to La Posada and my hip pain worsened as I waited for a decision between my Urologist and Orthopedist. Since the cancer hadn't Healed, I would also need major surgery to remove my bladder. They decided the hip should be first as it would need a shorter period of anesthetics. By then, my pain meds had affected my balance and coordination and I suffered several falls in our home. Finally, as I was being wheeled into surgery, Dr. Miller took Kris aside and said, "Your mother has been through hell the past two years, and I'm going to do my best to help her get well!" And that, he did!

> "Expect your every need to be met. Expect the answer to every problem. Expect abundance on every level. Expect to grow spiritually."
> –Anonymous

Suddenly, I was totally pain-free! The doctor was able to remove the old, loose appliance with just his thumb and forefinger. I don't remember details of that week in the hospital, but Kris tells me I walked to the bathroom without a cane, at last!

That was in July, 2010, and again I recuperated at La Hacienda with the help of their superb staff of nurses, Physical Therapists, and Occupational Therapists. When I was safe to walk again, I came back to our apartment with Skip and he no longer had to do my laundry, bring mail, etc... I was surrounded by wonderful Program women and friends from La Posada and Casa de Esperanza, where my six-year Board Member term included the last three years as President.

In between all these crises, I was also a member of the Planning Committee for our annual Green Valley Women's Conference. One time, we held a committee meeting in the dining room at La Hacienda, with me in a wheelchair! The Conference grew over the years to an attendance of nearly 300 women, and February, 2013 will mark our tenth anniversary.

Now I had to get back some stamina and good physical shape to prepare for the bladder removal scheduled for four months later, November 23rd, 2010. Unfortunately, my Urologist discovered those BCG treatments had shrunk my bladder to half its normal size, so I had to deal with incontinence as I waited. It was a terrible period.

> "Explore daily the will of God" –C.G. Jung

Finally, the surgical date came, two days before Thanksgiving of 2010. After a six-hour procedure, my "turkey drumstick" was a wet sponge on a stick! Then came the challenge of learning how and what I would be using as a substitute bladder the rest of my life. So, I moved back to La Hacienda for eight weeks this time, depending on Ostomy nurses to help train me and be sure of my capabilities before I finally came home. By then, my body had taken a great toll and my general health was very poor. My weight varied from 101-103, 30 pounds lighter than I had ever been. I am so grateful for my daughters who came to help me, and particularly, Skip, who was also very tired of this lonesome and worrisome routine.

"My sense of balance depends on my sense of humor." –Joan Malerba-Foran

After returning home, a visiting Ostomy nurse came twice a week to help train me with these new devices. I spent much time in bed, exhausted, but trying to slowly regain my strength and some weight! Skip was so patient and helpful through all of my crises and we were both doubly happy to have Fannie and Foxy to help us smile.

Once I felt strong enough, I decided to become a La Posada volunteer and find ways to "give back" for all the care, concern, kindness and love I received during all those months of illness and surgeries. I became a "grandma" with monthly visits and tea parties with preschoolers from the nearby Casa program. This also gave me the opportunity to teach those little ones my favorite song, "Sing a Rainbow." Additionally, I help with Bingo games on Saturdays at La Hacienda and at La Joya, the Assisted Living facility. I conduct weekly "News and Views" groups with residents. I continue to spend an hour there on Tuesday afternoons, facilitating a group on Trivia!

Otherwise, I am active with my AA family and have found myself wearing my old therapist hat at times, doing some pro-bono counseling with other women working to find their way through those early recovery challenges. I laughingly refer to two chairs at the *Posada Java* coffee shop here on campus as my "office!"

As I write all this, I am looking forward to our long-planned family reunion during the weekend of August 18, 2011. We will be celebrating my 80th birthday on the 17th (my impetus for writing this book), and Skip's and my 60th wedding anniversary will be just around the corner on September 8th!

BETTY FORD

Although I neglected to include my adventures with Betty (and Jerry) Ford in my earlier writing, I need to include some of that story, having recently returned from her funeral in Palm Desert. Soon after her Alcoholism Treatment Center experience in April, 1978, I met the medical director of that facility, Dr. Joseph Pursch at an Addictions Conference in Colorado. Knowing of my involvement and experience in addiction recovery, personally and professionally, he expressed to me his concern for Betty as the family would soon be arriving for their annual summers in Vail. He asked that I be a contact for her in Colorado as she as yet knew no-one for support at their mountain home. With three other AA women, we were invited to their home in Vail for dinner soon after their arrival. That was to be the beginning of a 30 year relationship with her and President Ford. We met annually in Vail for a three or four day get-together and then to their new home in Beaver Creek. They always entertained for dinner at their lovely round dining room table, festooned with beautiful centerpieces, and served delicious meals as our conversations covered many topics from politics to football! Shopping, talking, and eating covered the women's agenda after that and we shared many laughs, pictures, and attendance at different AA meetings in the Vail area.

Over the years, I visited the Fords in Rancho Mirage and was able to learn more about the Betty Ford Center which she "sponsored" and oversaw. Once, I was able to take Karen (during all her hip trauma) and I treasure the happy picture of her with Betty. Another time, Kim, who was working at the Scottsdale Center for the Arts, wanted to learn more about the McCallum Center for the Arts in Palm Desert. We stayed in the Ford's guest room and had great fun together, going through the closet where Betty stored all of her formal wear. Then, as we looked out the window early that morning, Kim was able to get a picture of Jerry doing his daily laps in the pool! So many lovely memories. And time goes on. My dear friend, Carole and I were able to attend Jerry's funeral in 2006, and we both recently returned from saying good-bye to Betty who died at age 93. I treasure several notes and book inserts written to me by Betty, and though I am sad at her loss, I am happy that she and Jerry are together again. She was buried next to him in Grand Rapids, on Jerry's birthday.

"What lies behind us and what lies before us are tiny matters, compared to what lies within us." –Ralph Waldo Emerson

Writing all these stories has been a cathartic adventure, being able to better define my periods of Feeling, Dealing, and Healing. Now, with over 44 years of recovery, I am forever grateful for being blessed with the Grace to endure and survive so many very painful times. This is all the result of learning to follow the guides for living found in the Twelve Steps, accompanied by the love and support of countless other AA peers, colleagues, my family and dear friends. Thank you, God!

> "My old habits have been discarded. I have no reason to pick them up today. The new me is here." –Anonymous

God, grant me the serenity

to accept the things I cannot change...

courage to change the things I can...

and wisdom to know the difference.

To be continued...

Mary Roush,
August, 2011

Living at La Posada in Green Valley, AZ (2008)

Volunteer Grandma

Karen with Betty Ford

EPILOGUE

Now, nearly a year after completing "my story," and before investigating what comes next, editing, picture copying, publishing, etc., I can add a few comments about events since August, 2011.

The long-planned family reunion was truly a happy memory maker, with 15 of us spending a weekend re-uniting, re-calling, re-living, and re-stating our love and commitment to each other. Our Saturday night banquet table was set for 16, including a special candle-lit place setting for Karen. We all had the opportunity to listen again to the cassette recording of very young Kathy and Karen reading their rendition of the *"Big Red"* children's book, bringing tears of laughter to everyone at the table.

Our family picture, taken after our dinner also included a life-size picture of Karen's face, which Kris held up among the other back row family members. The picture turned out to be a happy laugh-producing result as that image caught the camera's flash and there is no question of Karen's spirit shining through "all her family!" There is now a large display of all those pictures on a big box in the kitchen, which doubles as our refrigerator.

The holidays were quiet and enjoyable with friends and many fun events here at La Posada. Then, I found myself counting the days (weeks) anticipating another opportunity to attend the Academy Awards in late February. Kim invited me and Kay to be her guests and we each had fun shopping for dresses and making plans to meet and visit with Mike's family for two nights before finding our way high into the Hollywood Hills to stay at Kim's house. Then, at last, we were able to participate in the excitement of the red carpet adventure, followed by the amazing Awards production and the following Governors' Ball. Thank you again, Kim!

Currently, Skip is gradually regaining his stamina after some spinal surgery in February, followed in April by a mysterious intestinal illness which made it necessary for him to spend 15 days in La Hacienda (our back-up hospital). Happily, he is now much better, stronger, and taking fewer medications than before (!) with lower, more stable blood sugar numbers.

Granddaughter, Carrie has spent a great weekend visit with us, and has done so much to help me become less uncomfortable with the computer and SmartPhone!

I continue with my volunteer duties, and even participated in the La Posada annual Talent Show where I reprised my old *G.O.D. - Growing Old Disgracefully* - comedy routine in April. I also conduct a weekly "Trivia" group at the Assisted Living facility here as well as help conduct Bingo for La Hacienda residents on Saturday afternoons.

Our dear friends of 36 years, Carole and Bill Horton from Denver, spent another winter sojourn at their home in Green Valley, and as always, we shared many fun events with them. Carole and I have been so blessed to enjoy our deep and loving friendship all these years, as close as the sisters neither of us had been given in our earlier lives. Thank you, God!

Skip and I also participate in a 10-member discussion group: *"The Road We Travel,"* which enables all of us to share our thoughts and journeys as our days on this plane rapidly continue to dwindle.

Our wonderful adult children are living their own active and productive lives as well. Kathy is now a Psychiatric Nurse-Practitioner, living with her husband of 30 years, Alan, in Charlotte, North Carolina. Their 26 year-old daughter, Carrie will soon complete her two Master's Degrees at the seminary where Alan teaches.

Kris and her long-time partner, DD, live in Albuquerque where Kris, having achieved her Ph.D., teaches psychology at Central New Mexico Community College. She continues to maintain her private practice, conduct workshops, and now enjoys writing posts for her new self-development blog, www. MovedandShaken.com

Kim and her partner, Jeanne, live in Hollywood Hills, California. Kim earned her Master of Fine Arts at NYU. After a career in the Arts, she is now the Managing Director of Membership and Awards for the Academy of Motion Pictures, Arts and Sciences.

Mike decided to venture into the entertainment industry, working hard at becoming a screen writer and producer, with many intriguing projects resulting from his creative, imaginative mind. He lives with his family in Woodland Hills, California, where his wife, Susan, has her own home-based Public Relations and Advertising business. They just celebrated their 20th anniversary. Their son, Tom, 17, is a brilliant math/physics student, and Kate, nearly 15, is equally blessed and is a typical lovely social teenager.

Kay received her Business degree from the University of Colorado, as well as her Paralegal certification. Three years ago, she married Ricky and they live outside of Nashville in Columbia, Tennessee. She has had a very successful career with a law firm in Nashville for 10 years, and has recently been hired as the Administrative Assistant for the Nashville office of one of the country's largest mass-tort, class-action legal firms.

Since Karen "moved on," our spiritual growth seems to have sky-rocketed into whole new dimensions. She frequently continues to remind us of her presence by sending more yellow butterflies, and by turning on the lights in the ceiling fan above my desk...at the most "co-incidental" times! We continue to love and laugh, feeling her presence at all times. We are sure she had something to do with our finding and adoring our precious abandoned dogs, Foxy and Fannie! By the way, Native Americans believe that butterflies symbolize eternal life.

So, at last, my writing comes to an end and will hopefully find its way into book form to share with anyone who might find ways to identify and celebrate this opportunity to walk the walk set out for us by the God of our understanding through Feeling, Dealing, and Healing.

To sum it all up, "It's all about love!"

"Life is so much easier if you ride the horse the direction it's going" –Abraham Lincoln

80ᵗʰ Birthday Reunion with Granddaughters,
Carrie and Kate (2011)

"Growing Old Disgracefully" Skit (2012)

Made in the USA
Charleston, SC
09 April 2013